SPIRITUALITY

The Key to the Science of Theology

SPIRITUALITY
The Key to the Science of Theology

by PARLEY P. PRATT

CFI
Springville, Utah

First published in 1883 by Deseret News Company, Salt Lake City, Utah, and has now entered the public domain.

© 2007 Cedar Fort, Inc.

ISBN 13: 978-1-59955-116-6

Published by CFI, an imprint of Cedar Fort, Inc., 2373 W. 700 S., Springville, UT, 84663
Distributed by Cedar Fort, Inc., www.cedarfort.com

LIBRARY OF CONGRESS CATALOGING-IN-PUBLICATION DATA

Pratt, Parley P. (Parley Parker), 1807–1857.
  [Key to the science of theology]
  Spirituality : the key to the science of theology / Parley P. Pratt.
     p. cm.
  Originally published: Key to the science of theology. Salt Lake City :
Deseret News Steam Printing Establishment, 1874.
  ISBN 978-1-59955-116-6 (alk. paper)
  1. Church of Jesus Christ of Latter-day Saints—Doctrines. 2. Mormon
Church—Doctrines. 3. Spirituality—Church of Jesus Christ of Latter-day
Saints. 4. Spirituality—Mormon Church. I. Title.
  BX8635.3.P73 2007
  230'.93—dc22
                              2007040576

Cover design by Nicole Williams
Cover design © 2007 by Lyle Mortimer

Printed in the United States of America

10 9 8 7 6 5 4 3 2 1

Printed on acid-free paper

Designed as an introduction to the first principles of spiritual philosophy; religion; law and government; as delivered by the ancients, and as restored in this age, for the final development of universal peace, truth and knowledge.

—PARLEY P. PRATT

CONTENTS

FOREWORD

Parley Parker Pratt was converted to The Church of Jesus Christ of Latter-day Saints in 1830, the first year of its organization. He devoted his entire life to sharing the gospel and was martyred while serving a mission in Georgia in 1857, twenty-seven years following his baptism. He was one of the original Twelve Apostles called at the start of this dispensation and a close friend and associate of the Prophet Joseph Smith.

He was born on April 12, 1807, in Burlington, New York. Preston Nibley described Parley's early life in these words:

> His youth was spent on his father's farm, and he had little opportunity to gain an education. When he was nineteen he left home and moved westward to Ohio, where he obtained a small tract of forest land and constructed a log house. He then returned to New York and on September 9, 1827, was married to the sweetheart of his youth, Thankful Halsey. She accompanied him on his return to his "wilderness" home. In August, 1830, Parley P. Pratt and his wife decided to pay a visit to their parents in New York. At or near Rochester, Parley was given a copy of the Book of Mormon which had been published at Palmyra earlier in the year. He read the book with great interest and decided to seek out and interview the author. At Palmyra he met Hyrum Smith and sat up all night with him asking him questions about the new religion.[1]

Parley possessed a keen mind and a larger-than-life ability to express himself, especially in the written word. He was one of this dispensation's greatest orators and teachers of truth. When he first encountered the Book of Mormon, he eloquently described his experience and feelings:

> I opened it with eagerness, and read its title page. I then read the testimony of several witnesses in relation to the manner of its being found and translated. After this I commenced its contents by course. I read all day. Eating was a burden to me. I had no desire for food. Sleep was a burden when the night came, for I preferred reading to sleep. As I read, the Spirit of the Lord was upon me, and I knew that the book was true, as plainly as a man comprehends that he exists. My joy was now full. I determined to see the young man who had been the instrument of its discovery and translation.[2]

In the fall of 1830, Parley had the privilege of meeting the Prophet Joseph Smith for the first time.[3] For many years after this first meeting, he received tutilage from Joseph. At the first meeting they attended together, the Prophet invited Parley to speak. "I did so and afterward listened to a discourse from his own mouth, filled with intelligence and wisdom."[4]

Parley often commented on Joseph Smith's unique ability to touch hearts as he taught.[5] In fact, Elder Pratt was among the first, and one of the fortunate few, who were personally tutored by the Prophet Joseph Smith about the eternal principles of the restored gospel of Jesus Christ, and about the workings of the Spirit. While serving a mission with the Prophet Joseph Smith in the spring of 1834 through Ohio, Pennsylvania, and New York, Parley described these choice conversations: "As we journeyed day after day, and generally lodged together we had much sweet communion concerning the things of God and the mysteries of the Kingdom, and I received many admonitions and instructions which I shall never forget."[6]

When Joseph taught Parley for the first time about the real possibility for families to remain united throughout the eternities, it was as if the sun burst through clouds of darkness. Parley was able to learn firsthand from the Prophet the doctrines and blessings of eternal families.[7]

In 1838, when the Prophet Joseph and his brother Hyrum were arrested with Parley and others and imprisoned in Richmond, Missouri, Parley described one moment in that dungeon-like prison so clearly that all who have read it since feel as if they were there in person:

In one of those tedious nights we had lain as if in sleep until the hour of midnight had passed, and our ears and hearts had been pained while we had listened for hours to the obscene jests, the horrid oaths, the dreadful blasphemies and filthy language of our guards.

I had listened until I had become so disgusted, shocked, horrified, and so filled with the spirit of injustice that I could scarcely refrain from rising upon my feet and rebuking the guards; but had said nothing to Joseph or anyone else, although I lay next to him and knew he was awake. On a sudden he arose to his feet and spoke in a voice of thunder, or as a roaring lion, uttering as near as I can recollect the following words:

"Silence, ye fiends of the infernal pit! In the name of Jesus Christ, I rebuke you, and command you to be still. I will not live another minute and hear such language. Cease such talk, or you or I die this instant!"

He ceased to speak; he stood erect in terrible majesty; chained and without a weapon, calm, unruffled and dignified as an angel; he looked upon the quailing guards, whose weapons were lowered or dropped to the ground; whose knees smote together, and who, shrinking into a corner, or crouching at his feet begged his pardon, and remained quiet until a change of guards.

I have seen ministers of justice, clothed in magisterial robes, and criminals arraigned before them while life was suspended on a breath in the courts of England; I have witnessed a Congress in solemn session to give laws to nations; I have tried to conceive of kings, of royal courts, of thrones and crowns; but dignity and majesty have I seen but once, as it stood in chains, at midnight, in a dungeon in an obscure village of Missouri."[8]

Joseph's voice was raised in testimony to bless people as well. Again, Parley was there to observe the impression Joseph's testimony had on others. While traveling with Joseph Smith through Philadelphia, Parley listened and recorded as Joseph Smith bore personal witness of his First Vision and of the visitations of the angel Moroni. Parley described the impact that testimony had on a very large audience:

While visiting with brother Joseph in Philadelphia, a very large church was opened for him to preach in, and about three thousand people assembled to hear him. Brother Rigdon spoke first, and dwelt on the Gospel, illustrating his doctrine by the Bible. When he was through, brother Joseph arose like a lion about to roar; and being full of the Holy Ghost, spoke in great power, bearing testimony of the visions he had seen, the ministering of angels which he had enjoyed; and how he had found the plates of the Book of Mormon, and translated them by the gift and power of God. He commenced by saying: "If nobody else had the courage to testify of so glorious a message from Heaven, and of the finding of so glorious a record, he felt to do it in justice to the people, and leave the event with God."

The entire congregation were astounded; electrified, as it were, and overwhelmed with the sense of the truth and power by which he spoke, and the wonders which he related. A lasting impression was made; many souls were gathered into the fold. And I bear witness, that he, by his faithful and powerful testimony, cleared his garments of their blood. Multitudes were baptized in Philadelphia and in the regions around; while, at the same time, branches were springing up in Pennsylvania, in Jersey, and in various directions.[9]

Over years of friendship, discourses, missions, and enduring trials together, Elder Pratt had gleaned a substantial amount of knowledge from the Prophet Joseph Smith. The Prophet's teachings were so lucid and comprehensible that he felt Joseph had given the world a key that forever unlocked the gates leading to everlasting life. Joseph could describe our journey back to God with such clarity that his theology (the understanding of what God is like and how we might become even as he is) could be as easily studied and applied as any other science. Parley titled this work *A Key to the Science of Theology*. He began writing *A Key to the Science of Theology* in San Francisco in 1851, while serving a mission. Four years later, in March of 1855, the book was finally available to the public. This was the last book published by Parley prior to his martyrdom in 1857.

For over a century and a half, this book has stood as one of the most widely quoted doctrinal works on spirituality and the divine principle of revelation. In his preface, Parley summarized his intention for putting pen to paper:

> If the work proves an introductory key to some of the First Principles of the divine science of which it treats; if it serves to open the eyes of any of his fellow men, on the facts of the past, the present, and the future; if it leads to investigation and inquiry, and calls public attention to the greater and more particular truths which have been, or are about to be, revealed as a standard by which to unite the people of all nations and of all religions upon the rock, the sure foundation of divine, eternal, uncreated, infinite, and exhaustless Truth, it will have accomplished the end aimed at by the author.

A Key to the Science of Theology contained such a profound description of the first principles of the restored gospel of Jesus Christ, that in 1892 President Wilford Woodruff decided to place a copy of it next to the standard works inside the capstone of the Salt Lake Temple prior to lowering the statue of the angel Moroni on top of the capstone.[10] Today Moroni, with trumpet in hand, stands atop those testaments, calling to all the world to give heed to principles of salvation contained in the message of the Restoration. *A Key to the Science of Theology* by Parley P. Pratt is one of the Restoration's most powerful witnesses and truly does offer everyone on earth a key by which we may come to know who we are, eternally speaking, and learn how we might return to God's presence to experience eternal life and unending joy.

As Parley would bear witness in one of the hymns he wrote, the Restoration is real and it is gathering steam to fulfill its divinely appointed destiny:

The morning breaks; the shadows flee;
Lo, Zion's standard is unfurled!
The dawning of a brighter day, . . .
Majestic rises on the world.

The clouds of error disappear
Before the rays of truth divine;
The glory bursting from afar, . . .
Wide o'er the nations soon will shine. . . .

Jehovah speaks! let earth give ear,
And Gentile nations turn and live.
His mighty arm is making bare, . . .
His covenant people to receive.

Angels from heaven and truth from earth
Have met, and both have record borne;
Thus Zion's light is bursting forth . . .
To bring her ransomed children home.[11]

NOTES

1. *Stalwarts of Mormonism* (Salt Lake City: Deseret Book, 1954), 140–41.
2. *Autobiography of Parley P. Pratt,* edited by Parley P. Pratt Jr., Classics in Mormon Literature ed. (Salt Lake City: Deseret Book, 1985), 20.
3. See ibid., 47.
4. Ibid., 47.
5. See ibid., 32.
6. Ibid., 89.
7. See ibid., 260.
8. Ibid., 229.
9. Ibid., 260–61.
10. See Elder James E. Talmage, *The House of the Lord*, 126.
11. "The Morning Breaks," *Hymns*, no. 1.

PREFACE

by Parley Parker Pratt

The present is an age of progress, of change, of rapid advance, and of wonderful revolutions.

The very foundations of society—social, political, commercial, moral and religious—seem to be shaken as with a mighty earthquake, from center to circumference. All things tremble, creation groans, the world is in travail and pains to be delivered.

A new era has dawned upon our planet, and is advancing with accelerated force, with giant strides.

The railroads and the steamboats, with their progressive improvements in speed, safety and convenience, are extending and multiplying the means of travel, of trade, of association and intercommunication between countries whose inhabitants have been comparatively unknown to, or estranged from, each other.

But, as if even these means were too slow for the Godlike aspirations, the mighty throes of human thought, and its struggles for light and expansion, man seizes the lightning, tames and subdues it, and makes it the bearer of his thoughts and dispatches. While these things are in progress by one portion of mankind, another learns to seize and control a sunbeam, in a manner subservient to the progress of the fine arts, and by which means a man performs in a minute the work which a short time since would have employed the most active years of a lifetime.

While every science, every art is being developed; while the mind is awakened to new thoughts; while the windows of heaven are opened, as it were, and the profound depths of human intellect are stirred, moved from the foundation on all other subjects, religious knowledge seems at a standstill.

The *creeds* of the fathers seem to have been cast in the mold of other ages, to be adapted to a more narrow sphere of intellectual development, and to be composed of material too much resembling cast iron; or, at least, not sufficiently elastic to expand with the expansion of mind, to grow with the growth, and advance with the progressive principles of the age.

For these reasons, perhaps more than any other, the master spirits of the age are breaking loose from the old moorings and withdrawing from established and venerated systems, by which means society is distracted, divided, broken up, thrown, as it were, into a chaos of confused, disorganized individualization, without a standard or rallying point, without a nucleus by which to concentrate or reorganize this chaotic mass, these atoms of thought.

One thing is certain, according to ancient prophecy, and agreeable to the general expectation of this and other ages, the day approaches which will flood the earth with the pure principles of religious knowledge; a day when none will have to teach his neighbor, saying, Know ye the Lord; for all persons shall know him from the least to the greatest.

It should be a matter of serious thought and investigation—without respect to party, sect or creed, whether there should not, in the very nature of circumstances, and future Millennial hopes, be an entire remodelling, or re-organization of religious society, upon the broad basis of revealed knowledge, tangible fact, and philosophical, scientific and spiritual Truth—a universal "*standard,*" of immutable Truth, instead of numberless systems founded on uncertainty, opinion, mere human impression, or conjecture.

Can anything short of such a standard unite society, enlighten the world, establish real peace, brotherhood and fellowship, and put a final end to all religious ignorance, superstition, jargon, or discord? Is not a difference of opinion, or a disagreement on any given subject, a proof positive of existing ignorance, or want of light or information, on the part of the parties disagreeing? If so, the present age is certainly in the dark, or, in a great measure, ignorant on religious subjects. A knowledge of the Truth can alone bring the desired union and bid discord cease. If the Scriptures be true, it is not religious *opinion* which will cover the earth, and universally pervade every bosom, but it is a KNOWLEDGE, "The knowledge of God." "*God is Truth.*" To *know* him, is to know the Truth.

The present volume aims to embody, in a concise and somewhat original manner and style, a general view of the Science of Theology, as gathered from revelation, history, prophecy, reason and analogy.

If the work proves an introductory key to some of the first principles of the divine science of which it treats; if it serves to open the eyes of any of his fellow men, on the facts of the past, the present, and the future; if it leads to investigation and inquiry, and calls public attention to the greater and more particular truths which have been, or are about to be revealed as a standard by which to unite the people of all nations and of all religions upon the rock, the sure foundation of divine, eternal, uncreated, infinite and exhaustless Truth, it will have accomplished the end aimed at by the author.

CHAPTER ONE

Theology—Its Definition—Historical Illustration

Eternal Science! who would fathom thee
Must launch his hark upon a shoreless sea.
Thy knowledge yet shall overwhelm the earth;
Thy truth to immortality give birth,
Thy dawn shall kindle to eternal day,
And man, immortal, still shall own thy sway.

First. Theology is the science of communication, or of correspondence, between God, angels, spirits, and men, by means of visions, dreams, interpretations, conversations, inspirations, or the spirit of prophecy and revelation.

Second. It is the science by which worlds are organized, sustained, and directed, and the elements controlled.

Third. It is the science of knowledge, and the key and power thereof, by which the heavens are opened, and lawful access is obtained to the treasures of wisdom and intelligence—inexhaustible, infinite, embracing the past, the present, and the future.

Fourth. It is the science of life—endless and eternal, by which the living are changed or translated, and the dead raised.

Fifth. It is the science of *faith,* reformation, and remission of sins, whereby a fallen race of mortals may be justified, cleansed, and restored to the communion and fellowship of that Holy Spirit which is the light of the world, and of every intelligence therein.

Sixth. It is the science of spiritual gifts, by which the blind see, the deaf hear, the lame walk, the sick are healed, and demons are expelled from the human system.

Seventh. It is the science of all other sciences and useful arts, being in fact, the very fountain from which they emanate. It includes philosophy, astronomy, history, mathematics, geography, languages, the science of letters; and blends the knowledge of all matters of fact, in every branch of art, or of research. It includes, also, all the scientific discoveries and inventions—agriculture, the mechanical arts, architecture, shipbuilding, the properties and applications of the mariner's compass, navigation and music. All that is useful, great, and good; all that is calculated to sustain, comfort, instruct, edify, purify, refine or exalt intelligences; originated by this science, and this science alone, all other sciences being but branches growing out of *this—the root.*

Some of the facts stated in the foregoing, are beautifully illustrated in Theological history, of which the following is an imperfect summary—

God spake, and the worlds were framed by his word.

He spake, darkness dispersed, and light prevailed.

He commanded, and the elements—water and earth, separated, and assumed their proper bounds.

He commanded, and the earth brought forth vegetable and animal life in countless variety.

He commanded, and man, male and female, took upon them a tabernacle of flesh, and prepared to multiply and perpetuate their species in the new creation.

"The Lord God planted a garden," and thus introduced agriculture.

"He made coats of skins," hence the tailor's art.

The Lord God commanded and gave pattern for Noah's Ark, thus introducing the art of shipbuilding.

He revealed the patterns for the Tabernacle in the wilderness, with all its arrangements and furniture; and afterwards developed the entire plan and all the designs of that most stupendous of all works of art—the great Temple of Solomon, with all its furniture; thus developing and improving the art of architecture.

The Lord God wrote with his own finger on the "tables of Stone," on Mount Sinai; thus showing that the science of letters was cultivated and used by the highest Intelligence of the eternal heavens.

The Lord God has revealed by Ezekiel the Prophet, a plan for the survey and division of Palestine to the Twelve Tribes of Israel, on their return to the land of their fathers; also for laying out the new city of Jerusalem, with its squares, blocks, public grounds and suburbs, and its temple.

Thus Theology includes the surveyor's art, and the planning of cities, as well as temples, and shows that these arts are cultivated in heaven, and that the very highest Intelligence of the Heaven of heavens, stoops, or condescends, to grace these arts by his own particular attention and example.

In the Revelation of John the Apostle, on the Isle of Patmos, we have a specimen, a masterpiece, a climax of all that is great and grand in design, and splendid and glorious in execution, in cities, thrones, palaces, streets, pavements, outgrounds, gates, walks, squares, fountains, rivulets, gardens, fruits, groves, specimens or dress, poetry, song, music, marriage, bridal dress, feasting, books, literature, public worship, prophesying, prayer and praise, as existing in, and around the palaces of the New Jerusalem, the capital of heaven, the seat of government of the Eternal King.

The very gates of the city are numbered and named, together with the particular names of the precious stones forming the foundations thereof; the gold which composed the pavement of the streets—all are portrayed in the description.

And what is still more marvelous, all this surpassing grandeur of design, and stupendous wisdom and display in execution, were explored, comprehended, and described by a poor, illiterate fisherman, by the aid of the science and arts of Theology.

Having reviewed some of the works of the great Head—the President or First Teacher in the school of Theology, we will still continue the historic illustrations of this wonderful science, as developed and exemplified by the most eminent students and professors of the same.

By this science Adam obtained from his Father, the promise of the eternal dominion over the planet on which he was placed.

By this science Enoch overcame death, and ascended to a higher sphere of immortality and eternal life, without even being separated from his fleshly tabernacle.

By this science Noah foretold the flood, prepared to meet the event, and, with his family, survived the same, and became the greatest landed proprietor since Adam.

By the perversion and unlawful use of this science, King Nimrod built the stupendous Tower of Babel, but was frustrated, and his works were destroyed before their completion.

By this science various tongues and languages were instituted, and colonies—the germs of nations, planted beyond the seas and in all the earth.

By this science Abraham escaped the idolatry and priestcraft of the Egyptians, and of the world around him; obtained a good land secured to him and his seed by an immutable oath, covenant, and an everlasting, unchangeable title.

By this science he conversed with angels, and was favored with a personal interview with the Great Head and Founder of the science, who became his guest, and, after eating and drinking with him, blessed him and his wife, promised them an heir in their old age, and, finally, on parting, told him His design on Sodom and its neighborhood.

By this science Lot escaped the flames of Sodom, the knowledge being communicated by two angels.

By this science Isaac and Jacob also obtained promises and conversed with angels.

By it Joseph was exalted from a dungeon to a palace, for the salvation, from famine, of a nation and of his father's house.

By this science Moses performed his wonders in Egypt, in the Red Sea, and in the wilderness.

By the perversion and unlawful use of this science the magicians of Egypt withstood Moses for a time, and performed their enchantments.

By this science Joshua controlled the motions of the earth, and lengthened out the day by a simple command.

By this science the walls of Jericho were leveled with the earth, and the city was taken.

By this science the Jordan river was divided, while a nation crossed dry shod, to take possession of the promised land.

By this science Elijah controlled the heavens, that it rained not for three years and six months in Palestine. And by it he called forth and restored rain.

By it he overthrew the priests of Baal, and the kingdom of Ahab; put an end to the royal family of this idolatrous king, and placed Jehu on the throne.

By it he arose, like Enoch, to a higher sphere, without returning to dust.

By this science Samuel prophesied, raised up a mighty king and nation, and afterwards dethroned Saul and exalted an obscure shepherd boy to the throne of Israel.

By this science Isaiah, Jeremiah, Ezekiel, Daniel, and others, foretold the fate of Babylon, Egypt, Tyre, Jerusalem, and other cities and nations; and the exact career and final doom of Nebuchadnezzar, Belteshazzar, Cyrus, and other great and important personages, who were destined in turn to influence and decide the fate of nations.

By this science the furnace of fire was overcome, and the mouths of lions were closed, that no harm should befall the holy men of God.

By this science Zachariah, Elizabeth, John the Baptist, Simeon, Anna, Joseph, Mary, the wise men from the east, and the shepherds of Judea, enjoyed visions, communion with angels and the spirit of prophecy, so as to understand and welcome with joy the events of the birth and approaching ministry of Jesus Christ, when, as yet, all those not versed in this science, were in darkness on the subject, and as liable to reject the Savior as to receive Him.

Dreams and visions, enjoyed by means of this science, led and protected the Son of God in all his career of mortal life.

Finally—by this same power, a mighty angel descended, shook the earth, frightened the Roman guards, rolled away the great stone, broke the seal of the tomb, and called to life the sleeping body of Jesus Christ.

By this power the risen Jesus, eating, drinking, and conversing with his disciples, after his resurrection, commissioned and instructed them in the same science, ordained them to act in the same, and to impart its power to others, in all the world, with signs following them that believed.

By this science He ascended to the Father, and lives forever in the flesh, to shed forth the gifts and powers of the same science, according to his own will, and the will of his Father, to reign henceforth until He descends to the earth, conquers death in a last great conflict and puts all enemies under his feet.

By this same power his Apostles, being clothed with the full powers of the same on the day of Pentecost, ministered the powers and knowledge of this science to others, both Jew and Gentile, insomuch that the sick were healed, the blind saw, the dumb spake, the deaf heard, the lame walked, devils were cast out, and the dead were raised, while everywhere dreams, visions, the ministering of angels and the gift of prophecy were enjoyed.

CHAPTER TWO

Decline and Loss of This Science Among the Jews

O horrid, awful, melancholy sight!
A nation, wont to soar 'mid realms of light,
Degraded, fallen, sunk in dark despair,
The hiss, the scorn, the bye-word everywhere;
No eye to pity, and no arm to save,
Till wearied nature finds an exile's grave.

It now becomes our painful task to trace the decline of the science of Theology and its powers among the nations, and to review the awful consequences of such decline.

We will commence with the Jewish nation.

The science of Theology, as we have just reviewed, was enjoyed, and its powers were wonderfully developed, under the several dispensations called Patriarchal, Mosaic and Jewish.

There had, however, been a great decline, a retrogression of the powers and knowledge of the same previous to their restoration by John the Baptist and Jesus Christ.

This was owing to the general prevalence of sectarian principles, divisions, precepts, commandments, and doctrines of men, by which the law and the Prophets were made void, and a veil was thrown over them, or over the hearts of men, by which means they were misunderstood, or rather, not understood at all.

It therefore became the duty of Jesus Christ and his Apostles and Elders, as well as of his forerunner, to reprove those sects, denounce their

7

doctrines and traditions, and restore that which was lost in this great science.

This restoration was at first confined strictly to the nation of the Jews. But seeing they turned from it, and judged themselves unworthy of eternal life, preferring their own powerless forms and doctrines, to the science of revelation, miracles, visions, and prophecy, which had ever illuminated the pathway of their more ancient fathers, the Apostles turned from them, by the commandment of the Lord, and translated this science, with its keys and legitimate powers, to the Gentiles.

The nation had rejected and slain the Messiah, stoned the Prophets, and imprisoned and even murdered many of the Apostles and Elders; and Jesus had already, in tears of anguish, announced their doom—

"*O Jerusalem, Jerusalem, thou that killest the Prophets, and stonest them which are sent unto thee, how often would I have gathered thy children together, even as a hen gathereth her chickens under her wings, and ye would not! Behold, your house is left unto you desolate. For I say unto you, ye shall not see me henceforth till ye shall say, Blessed is He that cometh in the name of the Lord.*"

And again, on another occasion, the Messiah uttered his voice saying—"*There shall be great distress in the land, and wrath upon this people. And they shall fall by the edge of the sword, and shall be led away captive into all nations: and Jerusalem shall be trodden down of the Gentiles, until the times of the Gentiles be fulfilled.*"

Again he spake, concerning the Temple, saying—"There shall not be left here one stone upon another, that shall not be thrown down."

All these things, foretold by the science of Theology, were fulfilled in that generation. And Jerusalem has been destroyed, trodden down by the Gentiles, and the Jews have remained in captivity among the nations until now.

Our readers will readily discern the entire loss of the science and powers of Theology among this nation; the time, circumstances, and reasons of its decline, and the time or circumstances which will restore it unto them.

They lost it when, by the hand of the Apostles, it was taken from them and given to the Gentiles.

The result was, the destruction of their city and temple, and of their national existence.

Their temple, priesthood and offerings were no longer attended by divine power. Its outward forms were, therefore, of no possible use.

From that very time to the present—One thousand eight hundred and fifty-three of the Christian era, the voice of a Prophet has not been heard among the Jews.

Angels have not ministered unto them.

There has been no vision from the Lord.

No dream or interpretation.

No answer by Urim or Thummim.

No prophet.

No voice.

No sound.

No reproof.

No comforting whisper.

All is silence—stillness—solemn blackness of despair.

All is as the similitude and shadow of death.

Oh the weariness, the painful suspense, the watchings, the wanderings, the anxieties, the pains and sorrows of eighteen centuries! Oh the mist of ages which has shrouded a nation as it were in the gloom of an endless night!

When—O when, will their day dawn, and the day star of their ancient science appear above the horizon, disperse the cloud, and usher in the morning of a brighter day?

When they shall welcome a messenger in the name of the Lord.

When the times of the Gentiles are fulfilled.

CHAPTER THREE

The Progress, Decline, and Final Loss of the Science of Theology among the Gentiles—Foreshadowings of Its Restoration for the Ushering in of the Millennium

O Mystic Babel, long has been thy reign!
What direful evils follow in thy train!
The veil is rent—thy mystery revealed,
Angels cry wo! and God thy doom has sealed.
The nations, from thy long and dreary night,
Are waking now to everlasting light.

Returning to the Gentile Church, we find the science of Theology, with all its miraculous powers of visions, dreams, angels, revelations, prophecy, healings, etc., everywhere enjoyed. It had abated none of its powers, in its transition from Jew to Gentile. The wild branches, being engrafted into the good old stock, immediately partook of the root and fatness of the tame olive tree, and thus was produced the natural fruit.

But Paul, the great Apostle of the Gentiles, in his writings to the Romans, cautioned them to beware lest they should fall away after the same example as the Jews had done before them.

Said he—*"If God spared not the natural branches, take heed lest He also spare not thee."*

John the Apostle also predicted the rise and universal sway of a certain mystical power, a Babel of spiritual or religious confusion, in short—*"Mystery, Babylon the great, the mother of harlots and abominations of the earth."*

This power should bear rule among all nations. The kings and rulers of the earth should be drunken with the wine of her fornication. The merchants of the earth should become rich through the abundance of her delicacies.

This power should, according to the Prophet Daniel and Apostle John, "*wear out the Saints of the Most High;*" "*change times and laws;*" "*be drunken with the blood of the Saints, and with the blood of the martyrs of Jesus;*" "*destroy the mighty and the holy people;*" "*make war with the Saints, and overcome them*" until a set time.

All these predictions, and many others, foretell the doom of the Gentile Church, its destruction from the earth, and the consequent decline and cessation of the science of Theology, and of its powers and blessings in the Gentile world.

Connected with these predictions, we have the most positive prophetic declarations of Holy Writ concerning the overthrow and entire destruction of this same mystical power which had made war with the Saints.

Its judgments are set forth as far more terrible than those which befell Jerusalem. Plague, pestilence, sword, earthquake, and the flame of devouring fire will cause her to cease to be.

Then will usher in the Kingdom of our God, and the power of his Christ. Then will the Saints of the Most High take the Kingdom and the greatness of the Kingdom, under the whole heaven.

Thus are to be revived the ancient powers and blessings, the knowledge and wisdom of the science of Theology.

In the fulfillment of the foregoing predictions, the science of Theology declined, and passed away from among the Gentiles, just in proportion as the Church, or the Saints of the Most High, were warred against and overcome.

For years, centuries, ages, there had been no voice from heaven among the Gentiles, any more than among the Jews. They had fallen "*after the same example of unbelief,*" notwithstanding the caution of their great Apostle.

No Gentile Prophet had arisen and uttered his voice.

No kind angel had ministered to them.

No vision from the Lord.

No answer.

No inspired dream.

No voice.

No sound from the heavens.

No revelation has burst upon the silence of midnight darkness which has brooded over the nations.

Or, if such voice, such visions, such Prophet has occasionally burst forth with the testimony of Jesus, the spirit of prophecy, his testimony has been unheeded by the mass of the people called Christians, his voice silenced in death, or he and his followers have been banished from society, to wander in the mountains, forests, caves, or deserts of the earth; or, on the other hand, compelled to drag out an existence in the solitude of the dungeon.

Ages, centuries have passed, and Oh! what suffering! what torture! what rivers of tears! what oceans of blood! what groanings! what strong crying and tears on the earth! what prayers in heaven!

"How long, O Lord, holy and true, dost thou not judge and avenge our blood, on them that dwell on the earth?"

The fire consumed.

The sword devoured.

Hell's artillery bellowed.

Devils hugely grinned.

Widows and orphans mourned.

Heaven wept.

Saints prayed.

Justice stood aghast.

Mercy, retiring, dropped a tear of blood.

Angels, starting, half drew their glittering swords.

And the Gods, in solemn council, decreed a just vengeance.

Protest upon protest! reforms and re-reforms; revolutions, struggles, exertions of every kind, of mere human invention, have been tried, and tried in vain. The science of Theology, with all its keys and powers, once lost, could never, consistent with the ancient prophetic testimony, be restored to either Jew or Gentile, until the full time should arrive,—"*The times of restitution of all things, which God hath spoken by the mouth of all his holy prophets, since the world began.*"

The time for *a mighty angel to fly in the midst of heaven, having the everlasting Gospel to preach to them who dwell on the earth; to every nation, kindred tongue, and people.* (See John's revelation.)

The time of judgment for "*Mystery Babylon.*"

The times of "*the fullness of the Gentiles.*"

The times for the grafting in again of all the *natural branches of Israel.*

Then, and not till then, could this science, the keys, the powers of Theology, be restored to man.

No individual or combined human action could obtain or restore again these keys—this science.

A mighty angel held the keys of this science for the last days. A mighty angel was to restore the keys of the ancient Priesthood, Apostleship, power and blessings. A voice from heaven was to reveal the time, and send forth the cry—"*Come out of her my people, that ye be not partakers of her sins, and that ye receive not of her plagues. For her sins have reached unto heaven, and God hath remembered her iniquities.*"

All the darkness of the middle ages, all the priestcraft or kingcraft of every age, since the slaughter of the Apostles, all the oppressions, persecutions, or abuses of power, all the extravagances and idleness on the one hand, and all the sufferings and miseries of the toiling millions for want of the comforts of life on the other, all the ignorance, superstitions, errors, divisions and contentions which have transpired in the name of "*Christianity*" down to the present time; have been the results of the decline and loss of the keys and powers of the science of Theology, or for want of attention to them when existing on the earth.

Nor will the "*Christian*" world ever attain to any considerable degree of knowledge, power, or union in religious progress, until they discover their loss of this science, become sensible of the need of its restoration, and humble themselves as in the dust, and welcome a messenger who comes in the name of the Lord, with a commission from heaven, and with keys committed by the Angels of God—a new Apostolic commission, a restoration of the kingdom and Church, and power and gifts of God; a new dispensation, universally proclaimed in all the world, with power and signs following; and the whole consummated by the glorious restoration of Israel and Judah to their own land and nationality, and to the true fold of God; together with the second advent of Messiah and all his Saints with Him, to overthrow "Mystery Babylon," and reign on the earth.

Such are the events, such is the remedy for the past and present evils.

CHAPTER FOUR

Rise, Progress, Decline, and Loss of the Science of Theology on the Western Hemisphere, as Brought to Light by the Late Discovery of Ancient American Records

The spirit world is moved, the silence broken,
The ancient Seers from out the ground have spoken.
The appointed years on time's fleet wings have fled,
And voices whisper from the ancient dead.
Volumes of truth the sacred archives yield.
The past, the glorious future, stand revealed.

We are now, of necessity, carried back in our research to the cradle of nations, the Tower of Babel, in order to trace the history of this wonderful science, from the first emigration of a colony to the western hemisphere, till its final decline and overthrow, for the knowledge of which we are indebted to many ancient records, written by the fathers, or ancient students and professors of this science, on the western hemisphere.

Among these we will make honorable mention of the Prophets Jared, Ether, Lehi, Nephi, Mosiah, Alma, Abinadi, Mormon and Moroni, who wrote and prophesied in the Western Hemisphere, during the several ages intervening between the time of the dispersion at Babel, and the fifth century of the Christian era.

By the science of Theology Jared and his brother led a colony from the great tower to the sea coast, conversing with the Lord, and walking by the light of his revelations on the Way.

By this science they were instructed in the building of eight barges for uses similar to the ark of Noah.

By this science their leader saw God, face to face, and talked with him in plain humility, as one man talks with another, thus obtaining a knowledge of his future coming and Kingdom, and of the great events of all ages and generations.

By this science they were preserved on the great waters three hundred and forty-four days, and were then landed, with their eight barges, in the western hemisphere, together with their women, children, cattle, and seeds of every kind.

By this science they also became a great nation, peopling the entire continent, and enjoying all the blessings of civilization and heavenly light.

By the abuse and neglect of it they were at length exterminated, in the days of their Prophet Ether, who lived about six hundred years before Christ came in the flesh.

By this science the Prophets Lehi and Nephi came out with a colony from Jerusalem, in the days of Jeremiah the Prophet, and after wandering for eight years in the wilderness of Arabia, came to the sea coast, built a vessel, obtained from the Lord a compass to guide them on the way, and finally landed in safety on the coast of what is now called Chili, in South America.

By this science they also became a great nation, enjoyed many visions, had the ministering of angels, and of many prophets, by which means they knew of the coming, birth, ministry, death, resurrection, and ascension of Jesus Christ.

By this science they also enjoyed a personal visit from the risen Redeemer, who descended from heaven in their presence, taught them his Gospel, chose and ordained twelve of their number as Apostles, and prophesied many things.

By this science these twelve and others established the Gospel, Church and ordinances of God throughout the entire Western Hemisphere.

By this science their sick were healed, demons were expelled, the lame walked, the blind saw, the dumb spake, the deaf heard, and the dead were raised.

By this science three of those Apostles, having a change wrought upon them, tarried in the flesh upon the earth, ministered the Gospel and its blessings nearly four hundred years, and then withdrew from the people because of their iniquity, took away the keys of Apostleship and of the Gospel, and its powers, sealed up the records, and caused the work of healing, and of gifts and miracles, to cease from among the people, because of iniquity, bloodshed and persecution.

By this science they yet live in the flesh upon the earth, holding keys of Apostleship and power upon the western hemisphere, being now about one thousand eight hundred years old.

By this science (being held in reserve above the powers of mystery Babylon,) they will soon go forth, prophesying, preaching the Gospel, and doing mighty signs and wonders in the midst of all nations, in order to complete and mature the Gentile fullness, and restore the tribes of Israel. Nor is this all—John, the beloved disciple among the Jews, is yet alive in the flesh, and is held in reserve, to *prophesy again before many peoples, and nations, and tongues, and kings,* as it is written.

But to return to our history of the western hemisphere. After the science of Theology had ceased to be cultivated and enjoyed among this branch of Israel, terrible wars and bloodshed ensued. Governments and civilization were broken up, cities and countries were overthrown, all records and vestiges of truth were diligently sought and destroyed, as far as obtained.

And, finally, the whole face of the country was soaked, as it were, in blood, and strewed with the dead and dying.

The wild beasts of the forest and fowls of heaven devoured their flesh, and their bones were left to moulder unburied.

In other instances bodies were heaped up, and covered with mounds of earth.

All government became extinct, and the countries were overrun by tribes and bands of robbers at war with each other.

In this situation the records of Moroni leave them, in the fifth century of the Christian era, and much in the same situation, with some exceptions, the Europeans found them after a lapse of another thousand years.

Oh! who can contemplate the disgusting deformity, the dark features, the filthy habits, the idleness, the cruelty, the nakedness, the poverty, the misery, the sufferings, the ignorance of the descendants of this once favored branch of the royal blood of Abraham and Joseph, and not weep for very anguish, while his bosom yearns, and the fountains—the depths of his inmost soul, are stirred and moved within him!

Reader, *all these things have come upon them, on account of the abuses, the consequent decline and final loss of the keys and powers, of the science of Theology.*

But comfort your heart, their redemption is at the door.

CHAPTER FIVE

Keys of the Mysteries of the Godhead

Eternal Father, Being without end!
Thy glorious fullness who can comprehend!
Thine own infinitude alone is fraught
With attributes to swell a human thought,
To grasp thy knowledge, or thy nature scan,
As Father of the endless race of man.

"This is life eternal: to know the only true and living God, and Jesus Christ whom he hath sent."

S ince the decline of the science of Theology, a mystery, dark and deep, has shrouded the human mind, in regard to the person and nature of the Eternal Father, and of Jesus Christ, his Son.

Councils of the fathers, and wise men of Christendom, have assembled again and again, in order to solve the mystery of Godliness, and fix some standard or creed upon which all parties might rest and be agreed.

This, however, was not in their power. It is impossible for the world by its wisdom to find out God. *"Neither knoweth any man the Father, save the Son, and he to whomsoever the Son will reveal Him."*

The key to the science of Theology is the key of divine revelation. Without this key, no man, no assemblage of men, ever did, or ever will know the Eternal Father or Jesus Christ.

When the key of revelation was lost to man, the knowledge of God was lost. And as life eternal depended on the knowledge of God, of course the key of eternal life was lost.

Oh the mysteries, the absurdities, the contentions, the quarrels, the bloodshed, the infidelity, the senseless and conflicting theories which have grown and multiplied among sectaries on this subject!

Among these theories, we will notice one, which is, perhaps, more extensively received by different sects than any other. The language runs thus—"*There is one only living and true God, without body, parts or passions; consisting of three persons, the Father, Son, and Holy Ghost.*"

It is painful to the human mind to be compelled to admit that such wonderful inconsistencies of language or ideas, have ever found place in any human creed. Yet, so it is.

It is but another way of saying that there is a God who does not exist, a God who is composed of nonentity, who is the negative of all existence, who occupies no space, who exists in no time, who is composed of no substance, known or unknown, and who has no powers or properties in common with any thing or being known to exist, or which can possibly be conceived of, as existing either in the heavens or on the earth.

Such a God could never be seen, heard or felt by any being in the universe.

There never has been a visible idol worshipped among men, which was so powerless as this "*God without body, parts or passions.*"

The god of Egypt, the crocodile, could destroy.

The images of different nations could be felt and seen.

The Peruvian god, the Sun, could diffuse its genial warmth, light and influence.

But not so with the God without "*body, parts or passions.*"

That which has no parts has no whole.

Beings which have no passions, have no soul.

Before we can introduce the keys and powers of practical Theology to the understanding of men in this age, we must, of necessity, place within their comprehension some correct ideas of the true God.

It is written that, "*without faith it is impossible to please Him.*" Those who do not please him can never partake of the powers and gifts of the science of Theology, because the keys and powers of this science emanate from him as a free gift, but they are never given to those with whom He is not well pleased. The individual who would partake of this power must therefore have faith in Him. But how can he believe in a being of whom he has no correct idea?

So vague, so foreign from the simple, plain truth, are the ideas of the present age, so beclouded is the modern mind with mysticism, spiritual nonentity, or immateriality in nearly all of its ideas of the person or persons of the Deity, that we are constrained to use the language of the ancient Apostle, as addressed to the learned of Athens—"*Whom therefore ye ignorantly worship, him declare I unto you.*"

Although there are facts in our own existence which are beyond our present comprehension or capacity, which is true, in a higher sense, in relation to the Godhead, still the limited knowledge we are able to comprehend in relation to ourselves may at least be rational, and be as clearly conveyed and understood as any other subject. So with our knowledge of Deity. Although there are facts beyond our reach in relation to his existence, attributes and power, yet that which we may know and comprehend or express of Him, should be divested of all mystery, and should be as clearly conceived, expressed and conveyed as any other item of truth or of science.

Jesus Christ, a little babe like all the rest of us have been, grew to be a man, and "*received a fulness of the glory of the Father; and he received all Power, both in heaven and on earth; and the glory of the Father was with him, for he dwelt in him.*"

This man died, being put to death by wicked men.

He arose from the dead the third day, and appeared to his disciples. These disciples, on seeing him, supposed him to be a spirit only.

But their risen Lord adopted the most simple means of dispersing their *mysticism*, their *spiritual vagaries* or *immateriality*. He called upon them to handle him and see, "*For,*" said he, "*a spirit hath not flesh and bones, as ye see me have.*"

They accordingly handled Him, examined the prints of the nails in his hands and feet, and the mark of the spear in his side. But, as if this was not enough, in order to familiarize them still more with the facts of a material or tangible immortality, He ate and drank with them, partaking of a broiled fish and an honey-comb.

In short, He was with them for forty days, in which He walked, talked, ate, drank, taught, prophesied, commanded, commissioned, reasoned with and blessed them, thus familiarizing to them that immortality and eternal life which He wished them to teach in all the world.

He then ascended, in their presence, toward that planet where dwelt his Father and their Father, his God and their God.

While He was yet in sight in the open firmament, and they stood gazing upward, behold! two men stood by them in white raiment, and said:

"*Ye men of Galilee, why stand ye gazing up into heaven? This same Jesus, which is taken up from you into heaven, shall so come in like manner as ye have seen him go into heaven.*"

Here, then, we have a sample of an immortal God—a God who is often declared in the Scriptures to be like his Father, "*being the brightness of his glory, and the express image of his person,*" and possessing the same attributes as his Father, in all their fullness; a God not only possessing body and parts, but flesh and bones, and sinews, and all the attributes, organs, senses and affections of a perfect man.

He differs in nothing from his Father, except in age and authority, the Father having the seniority, and, consequently, the right, according to the patriarchal laws of eternal Priesthood, to preside over Him, and over all his dominions, forever and ever.

While on the one hand, this God claims affinity and equality, as it were, with his Father, He claims on the other hand, affinity and equality With his brethren, on the earth, with this difference, however, that his person is a specimen of Divine, eternal Humanity, immortalized, and with attributes perfected; while his brethren who dwell in mortal flesh, although children of the same royal Parent in the heavens, are not yet immortalized, as it regards their fleshy tabernacles, and are not perfected in their attributes; and although joint heirs, are younger, He being the first born among many brethren in the spiritual world. They are therefore subject to Him.

But every man who is eventually made perfect—raised from the dead, and filled or quickened with a fullness of celestial glory, will become like them in every respect, physically and in intellect, attributes or powers.

The very germs of these Godlike attributes, being engendered in man, the offspring of Deity, only need cultivating, improving, developing and advancing by means of a series of progressive changes, in order to arrive at the fountain "*Head,*" the standard, the climax of Divine Humanity.

The difference between Jesus Christ and his Father is this—one is subordinate to the other, does nothing of Himself, independently of the Father, but does all things in the name and by the authority of the Father, being of the same mind in all things. The difference between Jesus Christ and another immortal and celestial man is this—the man is subordinate to Jesus Christ, does nothing in and of himself, but does all things in the name of Christ, and by his authority, being of the same mind, and ascribing all the glory to his Father.

On account of the double relationship of Jesus Christ—with God the Father on one hand, and with man on the other, many have adopted the creed that, "*Two whole and perfect natures*" were blended in the person of Jesus Christ; that He was every way a God, and every way a man; as if God and man were two distinct species. This error came by reason of not knowing ourselves. For just in proportion as we comprehend ourselves in our true light, and our relationships and affinities with the past, present and future, with time and eternity, with Gods, angels, spirits and men, who have gone before us, and who will come after us, so, in proportion, we may be able to benefit by the keys of the mysteries of the Godhead, or in other words, to know and comprehend Jesus Christ and his Father.

Gods, angels and men are all of one species, one race, one great family, widely diffused among the planetary systems, as colonies, kingdoms, nations, etc.

The great distinguishing difference between one portion of this race and another, consists in the varied grades of intelligence and purity, and also in the variety of spheres occupied by each, in the series of progressive being.

An immortal man, possessing a perfect organization of spirit, flesh and bones, and perfected in his attributes, in all the fullness of celestial glory, is called *a God.*

An immortal man, in progress of perfection, or quickened with a lesser degree of glory, is called *an angel.*

An immortal spirit of man, not united with a fleshly tabernacle, is called a spirit.

An immortal man, clothed with a mortal tabernacle, is called a man.

It may then consistently enough be said, that there are, in a subordinate sense, a plurality of Gods, or rather of the sons of God; although there is one Supreme Head, who is over all, and through all, and in all his sons, by the power of his Spirit.

Jesus Christ and his Father are two persons, in the same sense as John and Peter are two persons. Each of them has an organized, individual tabernacle, embodied in material form, and composed of material substance, in the likeness of man, and possessing every organ, limb and physical part that man possesses.

There is no more mystery connected with their oneness, than there is in the oneness of Enoch and Elijah, or of Paul and Silas.

Their oneness consists of a oneness of spirit, intelligence, attributes, knowledge or power.

If Enoch, Elijah, Abraham, Peter, Paul, and millions of others ever attain to the immortal life, and their fleshly tabernacles be quickened by a fullness of celestial life and light, intelligence and power, then it can be said of them, *they are one, as the Father and the Son are one.*

It could then be said of each of them, in him dwells all the fullness of the powers and attributes of the Eternal God, or, in other words, he possesses endless life, together with all intelligence, knowledge, light and power.

He therefore has the same mind as all the others—is in communication and in perfect union with each, and all of them.

All these are Gods, or sons of God—they are the Kings, Princes, Priests and Nobles of Eternity. But over them all there is a Presidency or Grand Head, who is the Father of all. And next to him is Jesus Christ, the eldest born, and first heir of all the realms of light.

Every person knows, by reflection, that intelligence may be imparted without diminishing the store possessed by the giver. Therefore it follows, that millions of individual beings may each receive, all the attributes of eternal life, and light, and power.

Again it follows, that in the use of this power, by consent and authority of the Head, any one of these Gods may create, organize, people, govern, control, exalt, glorify, and enjoy worlds on worlds, and the inhabitants thereof; or, in other words, each of them can find room in the infinitude of space, and unoccupied chaotic elements in the boundless storehouse of eternal riches, with which to erect for himself thrones, principalities and powers, over which to reign in still increasing might, majesty and dominion, for ever and ever.

All these are kingdoms, together with their Kings, are in subordination to the great Head and Father of all, and to Jesus Christ the first born, and first heir, among the sons of God.

All these kingdoms, with all their intelligences, are so many acquisitions to his dominion who is Lord of lords and King of kings, and of whom it is written by the Prophet Isaiah, *"of the increase of his kingdom there shall be no end."*

All these are so many colonies of our race, multiplied, extended, transplanted and existing for ever and ever, as occupants of the numberless planetary systems which do now exist, or which will roll into order, and be peopled by the operations of the Holy Spirit, in obedience to the mandates of the sons of God.

These kingdoms present every variety and degree in the progress of the great science of life, from the lowest degradation amid the realms of death, or the rudimental stages of elementary existence, upward through all the ascending scale, or all the degrees of progress in the science of eternal life and light, until some of them in turn rise to thrones of eternal power.

Each of these Gods, including Jesus Christ and his Father, being in possession of not merely an organized spirit, but a glorious immortal body of flesh and bones, is subject to the laws which govern, of necessity, even the most refined order of physical existence.

All physical element, however embodied, quickened or refined, is subject to the general laws necessary to all existence.

Some of these laws are as follows—

First. Each atom, or embodiment of atoms, necessarily occupies a certain amount of space.

Second. No atom, or embodiment of atoms, can occupy the identical space occupied by other atoms or bodies.

Third, Each individual organized intelligence must possess the power of self-motion to a greater or less degree.

Fourth. All voluntary motion implies an inherent will, to originate and direct such motion.

Fifth. Motion, of necessity, implies that a certain amount of time is necessary in passing from one portion of space to another.

These laws are absolute and unchangeable in their nature, and apply to all intelligent agencies which do or can exist.

They, therefore, apply with equal force to the great, supreme, Eternal Father of the heavens and of the earth, and to his meanest subjects.

It is, therefore, an absolute impossibility for God the Father, or Jesus Christ, to be everywhere personally present.

The omnipresence of God must therefore be understood in some other way than of his bodily or personal presence.

The Holy Ghost is the third member of the Godhead and is also a personage, but a personage of Spirit which does not have a body of flesh and bones. The mission of the Holy Ghost is to partake of the things of the Father and the Son and teach them unto those who have received the gift of the Holy Ghost by the laying on of hands. He guides the true disciples in all truth, shows them things to come, reveals the past and makes known the hidden treasures of the kingdom of God. This Spirit is also called the Comforter which the world cannot receive and which the Savior promised to send to his disciples after he ascended into heaven.

This leads to the investigation of that substance called the Holy Spirit, or Light of Christ. This Spirit "giveth light to every man that cometh into the world and the spirit enlighteneth every man through the world, that hearkeneth to the voice of the Spirit."

As the mind passes the boundaries of the visible world, and enters upon the confines of the more refined and subtle elements, it finds itself associated with certain substances in themselves invisible to our gross organs, but clearly manifested to our intellect by their tangible operations and effects.

The very air we breathe, although invisible to our sight, is clearly manifested to our sense of feeling. Its component parts may be analyzed. Nay more, the human system itself is an apparatus which performs a chemical process upon that element. It is received into the system by the act of respiration, and there immediately undergoes the separation of its component parts.

The one part, retained and incorporated in the animal system, diffuses life and animation, by supplying the necessary animal heat, etc., while the other part, not adapted to the system, is discharged from the lungs to mingle with its native element.

There are several of these subtle, invisible substances but little understood as yet by man, and their existence is only demonstrated by their effects. Some of them are recognized under several terms, electricity, galvanism, magnetism, animal magnetism, spiritual magnetism, essence, spirit, etc.

The purest, most refined and subtle of all these substances, and the one least understood, or even recognized, by the less informed among mankind, is that substance called the Holy Spirit.

This substance, like all others, is one of the elements of material or physical existence, and therefore subject to the necessary laws which govern all matter, as before enumerated.

Like the other elements, its whole is composed of individual particles. Like them, each particle occupies space, possesses the power of motion, requires time to move from one part of space to another, and can in no wise occupy two spaces at once. In all these respects it differs nothing from all other matter.

This substance is widely diffused among the elements of space. This Holy Spirit, under the control of the Great Eloheim, is the grand moving cause of all intelligences, and by which they act.

This is the great, positive, controlling element of all other elements. It is omnipresent by reason of its infinitude of its particles, and it comprehends all things.

It is the agent or executive, by which God organizes and puts in motion all worlds, and which, by the mandate of the Almighty, or any of his commissioned servants performs all the mighty wonders, signs and miracles ever manifested in the name of the Lord, the dividing of the sea, the removing of a mountain, the raising of the dead, or the healing of the sick.

Those beings who receive of its fullness are called sons of God, because they are perfected in all its attributes and powers, and, being in communication with it, can, by its use, perform all things.

Those beings who receive not a fullness, but a measure of it, can know and perform some things, but not all.

This is the true light, which in some measure illuminates all men. It is, in its less refined existence, the physical light which reflects from the sun, moon, and stars, and other substances; and by reflection on the eye, makes visible the truths of the outward world.

It is, also, in its higher degrees, the intellectual light of our inward and spiritual organs, by which we reason, discern, judge, compare, comprehend and remember the subjects within our reach.

Its inspiration constitutes instinct in animal life, reason in man, vision in the Prophets, and is continually flowing from the Godhead throughout all his creations.

God sits enthroned in the midst of all his creations, and is filled and encircled with light unapproachable by those of the lower spheres.

He associates with myriads of his own begotten sons and daughters who, by translation or resurrection, have triumphed over death.

His ministers are sent forth from his presence to all parts of his dominions.

His Holy Spirit centers in his presence, and communicates with and extends to the utmost verge of his dominions, comprehending and controlling all things under the immediate direction of his own will, and the will of all those in communication with him, in worlds without end.

CHAPTER SIX

Origin of the Universe

Boundless infinitude of time, and space.
And elements eternal! Who can trace
Earth with its treasures, Heaven with its spheres,
Time's revolutions, eternity's years?
But what are all these, when measured by thee,
But marks on thy dial, or motes on thy sea?

The idea of a God without "body, parts or passions," is not more absurd or inconsistent than that modern popular doctrine, that all things were created from nonentity, or, in other words, that something originated from nothing.

It is a self-evident truth, which will not admit of argument, that nothing remains nothing. Nonentity is the negative of all existence. This negative possesses no property or element upon which the energies of creative power can operate.

This mysticism must, therefore, share the fate of the other mysteries of false Theology and philosophy, which have for ages shrouded the world in the sable curtains of a long and dreary night. It must evaporate and disappear as a mere creation of fancy, while in its place, are introduced the following self-evident and incontrovertible facts—

First. There has always existed a boundless infinitude of space.

Second. Intermingled with this space there exist all the varieties of the elements, properties, or things of which intelligence takes cognizance; which elements or things taken altogether compose what is called Universe.

29

Third. The elements of all these properties or things are eternal, uncreated, self-existing. Not one particle can be added to them by creative power. Neither can one particle be diminished or annihilated.

Fourth. These eternal, self-existing elements possess in themselves certain inherent properties or attributes, in a greater or less degree; or, in other words, they possess intelligence, adapted to their several spheres.

These elements have been separated, by philosophers, into two grand divisions, viz.;—

Physical and Spiritual."

To a mind matured, or quickened with a, fullness of intelligence, so as to be conversant with all the elements of nature, there is no use for the distinction implied in such terms.

To speak more philosophically, all the elements are spiritual, all are physical, all are material, tangible realities. Spirit is matter, and matter is full of spirit. Because all things which do exist are eternal realities, in their elementary existence.

Who then can define the precise point, in the scale of elementary existence, which divides between the physical and spiritual kingdoms? There are eyes which can discern the most refined particles of elementary existence. There are hands and fingers to whose refined touch all things are tangible.

In the capacity of mortals, however, some of the elements are tangible, or visible, and others invisible. Those which are tangible to our senses, we call physical: those which are more subtle and refined, we call spiritual.

Spirit is intelligence, or the light of truth, which filleth all things.

Its several emotions or affections, such as love, joy, etc., are but so many actions or motions of these elements, as they operate in their several spheres.

By these actions or emotions the elements manifest their eternal energies, attributes, or inherent powers.

In contemplating the works of creation, then, the student must not conceive the idea that space, or time or element or intelligence was originated, but rather that these are eternal, and that they constitute the energies which act, and the things acted upon, including the place and time of action.

The whole vast structure of universal organized existence presents undeniable evidence of three facts, viz.—

First. The eternal existence of the elements of which it is composed.

Second. The eternal existence of the attributes of intelligence, and wisdom to design.

Third. The eternal existence of power to operate upon and control these eternal elements, so as to carry out the plans of the designer.

It will be recollected that the last chapter recognizes a family of Gods, or, in other words, a species of beings, who have physical tabernacles of flesh and bones, in the form of man, but so constructed as to be capable of eternal life; that these tabernacles are quickened, or animated by a fullness of that holiest, of all elements, which is called the Holy Spirit, which element or spirit, when organized, in individual form, and clothed upon with flesh and bones in the highest possible refinement, contains, in itself, a fullness of the attributes of light, intelligence, wisdom, love, and power; also that not organized in bodily forms, but widely diffused among the other elements of space.

A General Assembly, Quorum or Grand Council of the Gods, with their President at their head, constitute the designing and creating power.

The motive power, which moves to action this grand creative power, is wisdom, which discovers a use for all these riches, and inspires the carrying out of all the designs in an infinite variety of utility and adaptation.

Wisdom inspires the Gods to multiply their species and to lay the foundation for all the forms of life, to increase in numbers, and for each to enjoy himself in the sphere to which he is adapted, and in the possession and use of that portion of the elements necessary to his existence and happiness.

In order to multiply organized bodies, composed of spiritual element, worlds and mansions composed of spiritual element would be necessary as a home, adapted to their existence and enjoyment. As these spiritual bodies increased in numbers, other spiritual worlds would be necessary, on which to transplant them.

Again. In order to enable these organized spirits to take upon them a fleshly tabernacle, physical worlds, with all their variety and fullness, would be necessary for their homes, food, clothing, etc., that they might live, die, and rise again to receive their inheritances on their respective earths.

Hence the great work of regeneration of worlds, or the renovation and adaptation of the elements to the resurrection and eternal state of man, would also be endless, or eternally progressive.

Through every form of life, and birth, and change, and resurrection, and every form of progress in knowledge and experience, the candidates for eternal life must look upon the elements as their home; hence the elements, upon the principle of adaption, must keep pace with the possessors who use them, in all the degrees of progressive refinement.

While room is found in infinite space:

While there are particles of unorganized element in Nature's storehouse:

While the trees of Paradise yield their fruits, or the Fountain of Life its river:

While the bosoms of the Gods glow with affection:

While eternal charity endures, or eternity itself rolls its successive ages, the heavens will multiply, and new worlds and more people be added to the kingdoms of the Fathers.

Thus, in the progress of events, unnumbered millions of worlds and of systems of worlds will necessarily be called into requisition, and be filled by man, and beast, and fowl, and tree, and all the vast varieties of beings and things which ever budded and blossomed in Eden, or thronged the hills and valleys of the celestial Paradise.

When, in the endless progression of events, the full time had arrived for infinite wisdom to organize and people this globe which we inhabit, the chaotic elements were arranged in order. It appears, at the commencement of this grand work, that the elements, which are now so beautifully arranged and adapted to vegetable and animal life, were found in a state of chaos, entirely unadapted to the uses they now serve.

There was one vast mixture of elements. Earth, water, soil, atmosphere—in short, the entire elements of which this mass was composed seem to have been completely compounded or mingled into one vast chaos, and the whole overwhelmed with a darkness so dense as to obscure the light of heaven.

Let us turn from the contemplation of scenes so sublimely fearful. Suffice it to say, the mandate came, darkness fled, the veil was lifted, light pierced the gloom, and chaos was made visible. Oh what a scene! A world without landscape, without vegetation, without animal life, without man or animated beings. No sound broke on the stillness, save the voice of the moaning winds and of dashing, foaming waters. Again, a voice comes booming over the abyss, and echoing amid the wastes, the mass of matters hears and trembles, and lo! the sea retires, the muddy, shapeless mass lifts its head above the waters.

Molehills to mountains grow. Huge islands next appear, and continents at length expand to view, with hill and vale, in one wide, dreary waste, unmeasured and untrodden.

The surface, warmed and dried by the cheering, rays of the now resplendent sun, is prepared for the first seeds of vegetation.

A Royal Planter now descends from yonder world of older date, and bearing in his hand the choice seeds of the older Paradise, he plants them in the virgin soil of our new-born earth. They grow and flourish there, and, bearing seed, replant themselves, and thus clothe the naked earth with scenes of beauty and the air with fragrant incense. Ripening fruits and herbs at length abound. When lo! from yonder world is transferred every species of animal life. Male and female, they come, with blessings on their head; and a voice is heard again, *Be fruitful and multiply.*

Earth, its mineral, vegetable and animal wealth—its Paradise, prepared, down comes from yonder world on high, a Son of God, with his beloved spouse. And thus a colony from heaven, it may be from the sun, is transplanted on our soil. The blessings of their Father are upon them, and the first great law of heaven and earth is again repeated, "Be fruitful and multiply."

Hence the nations which have swarmed our earth.

In after years, when Paradise was lost by sin; when man was driven from the face of his heavenly Father, to toil, and droop, and die; when heaven was veiled from view; and, with few exceptions, man was no longer counted worthy to retain the knowledge of his heavenly origin; then, darkness veiled the past and future from the heathen mind; man neither knew himself, from whence he came, nor whither he was bound. At length a Moses came, who knew his God, and would fain have led mankind to know him too, and see him face to face. But they could not receive his heavenly laws, or bide his presence.

Thus the holy man was forced again to veil the past in mystery, and in the beginning of his history, assign to man an earthly origin.

Man, moulded from the earth, as a brick!

Woman, manufactured from a rib!

Thus, parents still would fain conceal from budding manhood the mysteries of procreation, or the sources of life's ever-flowing river, by relating some childish tale of new born life, engendered in the hollow trunk of some old tree, or springing with spontaneous growth like mushrooms from out the heaps of rubbish. O man! When wilt thou cease to be a child in knowledge?

Man as we have said, is the offspring of Deity. The entire mystery of the past and future, with regard to his existence, is not yet solved by mortals.

We first recognize him, as an organized individual or intelligence, dwelling with his Father in the eternal mansions. This organized spirit we call a body, because, although composed of the spiritual elements, it possesses every organ after the pattern, and in the likeness or similitude of the outward or fleshly tabernacle it is destined eventually to inhabit. Its organs of thought, speech, sight, hearing, tasting, smelling, feeling, etc., all exist in their order as in the physical body; the one being the exact similitude of the other.

This individual, spiritual body, was begotten by the Heavenly Father, in his own likeness and image, and by the laws of procreation.

It was born and matured in the heavenly mansions, trained in the school of love in the family circle, and amid the most tender embraces of parental and fraternal affection.

In this primeval probation, in its heavenly home, it lived and moved as a free and rational intelligence, acting upon its own agency, and, like all intelligence, independent in its own sphere. It was placed under certain laws and was responsible to its great Patriarchal Head.

This has been called a "first estate." And it is intimated that of the spirits thus placed upon their agency, one-third failed to keep their first estate, and were thrust down and reserved in chains of darkness, for future judgment. As these are not permitted to multiply their species, or to move forward in the scale of progressive being, while, in this state of bondage and condemnation, we will trace them no further, as their final destiny is not revealed to mortals.

The spirits which kept their first estate, were permitted to descend below, and to obtain tabernacles of flesh in the rudimental existence in which we find them in our present world, and which we will call a second estate.

In passing the veil which separates the first and second estates, man becomes unconscious, and on awakening in his second estate, a veil is wisely thrown over all the past.

In his mortal tabernacle he remembers not the scenes, the endearing associations, of his first primeval childhood in the heavenly mansions. He therefore commences anew in the lessons of experience, in order to start on a level with the new born tabernacle, and to redevelop his intellectual faculties in a progressive series, which keep pace with the development of the organs and faculties of the outward tabernacle.

During his progress in the flesh, the Holy Spirit may gradually awaken his faculties; and in a dream or vision, or by the spirit of prophecy, reveal, or rather awaken the memory to a partial vision, or to a dim and half defined recollection of the intelligence of past. He sees in part, and he knows in part; but never while tabernacled in mortal flesh will he fully awaken to the intelligence of his former estate. It surpasses his comprehension, is unspeakable and even unlawful to be uttered.

Having kept his second estate and filled the measure of his responsibilities in the flesh, he passes the veil of death, and enters a third estate, or probationary sphere. This is called a world of spirits, which will be treated on more fully under its appropriate head.

Filling the measure of his responsibilities in the world of spirits, he passes by means of the resurrection of the body, into his fourth estate, or sphere of human existence. In this sphere he finds himself clothed upon with an eternal body of flesh and bones, with every sense and every organ restored and adapted to their proper use.

He is thus prepared with organs and faculties adapted to the possession and enjoyment of every element of the physical and spiritual worlds, which can gratify the senses, or conduce to the happiness of intelligences. He associates, converses, loves, thinks, acts, moves, hears, tastes, smells, eats, drinks and possesses.

In short, all the elements necessary to his happiness, being purified, exalted and adapted to the sphere in which he exists, are placed within his lawful reach, and made subservient to his use.

CHAPTER SEVEN

Destiny of the Universe

The mystic future, with its depths profound,
For ages counted as forbidden ground,
Now lifts its veil, that man may penetrate
The secret springs, the mysteries of fate;
Know whence he is, and whither he is bound
And why the spheres perform their ample round.

The Grand Council having developed the vast structure of the heavens and the earth, with all their fullness, with the evident design of utility and adaptation to certain definite uses, it well becomes us to watch their progress, and to study with diligence their future and final destiny.

From a general traditional belief in an immaterial hereafter, many have concluded that the earth and all material things would be annihilated as mere temporary structures: that the material body, and the planet it occupies, make no part of eternal life and being; in short, that God, angels, and men, become at last so lost, dissolved, or merged in spirituality or immateriality, as to lose all adaptation to the uses of the physical elements; that they will absolutely need no footstool, habitation, possession, mansion, home, furniture, food, or clothing; that the whole vast works and beautiful designs of the visible creation are a kind of necessary evil or clog on the spiritual life, and are of no possible use except to serve for the time being for the home and sustenance of beings in their grosser or rudimental state.

What a doleful picture! With what gloom and melancholy must intelligences contemplate the vast structure as viewed in this light!

What a vastness of design!

What a display of wisdom!

What a field of labor in execution, do the works of creation present to the contemplative mind!

Yet all this wisdom of design, all this labor of execution, after serving a momentary purpose, to be thrown away as an incumbrance to real existence and happiness!

All these "spiritual," "immaterial" vagaries have no foundation in truth.

The earth and other systems are to undergo a variety of changes in their progress towards perfection. Physical and spiritual elements are the agents of these changes. But it is an eternal, unchangeable fact, a fixed law of nature, easily demonstrated and illustrated by chemical experiment, that no active force or potent element can annihilate a particle of matter, to say nothing of a whole globe.

A *new heaven and a new earth* are promised by the sacred writers. Or, in other words, the planetary systems are to be changed, purified, refined, exalted and glorified, in the similitude of the resurrection, by which means all physical evil or imperfection will be done away.

In their present state they are adapted to the rudimental state of man. They are, as it were, the nurseries for man's physical embryo formation. Their elements afford the means of nourishing and sustaining the tabernacle, and of engendering and strengthening the organ of thought and mind, wherein are conceived and generated thoughts and affections which can only be matured and consummated in a higher sphere—thoughts pregnant with eternal life and love.

As the mind enlarges, the aspirations of an eternal being once ennobled and honored in the councils of heaven, among the sons of God, reach forth too high, and broad, and deep, to be longer adapted to the narrow sphere of mortal life. His body is imprisoned, chained to the earth, while his mind would soar aloft and grasp the intelligence, wisdom and riches of the boundless infinite.

His rudimental body must therefore pass away, and be changed so as to be adapted to a wider and more glorious sphere of locomotion, research, action, and enjoyment.

When the planet on which he dwells has conceived, brought forth and nourished the number of tabernacles assigned to it in its rudimental state, by infinite wisdom, it must needs be acted upon by a chemical process. The purifying elements; for instance, fire, must needs be employed to bring it through an ordeal, a refinement, a purification, a change commensurate with that which had before taken place in the physical tabernacles of its inhabitants. Thus renovated, it is adapted to resurrected man.

When man, and the planet on which he lives, with all its fullness, shall have completed all their series of progressive changes, so as to be adapted to the highest glories of which their several characters and species are capable, then, the whole will be annexed to, or numbered with the eternal heavens, and will there fulfill their eternal rounds, being another acquisition to the mansions or eternally increasing dominions of the great Creator and Redeemer.

Worlds are mansions for the home of intelligences.

Intelligences exist in order to enjoy.

Joy, in its fullness, depends on certain principles, viz.—Life Eternal. Love Eternal. Peace Eternal. Wealth eternal. etc.

Without the first, enjoyment lacks durability.

Without the second, it can hardly be said to exist.

Without the third, it would not be secure.

Without the fourth, it must be limited, etc.

Eternal life, in its fullness, implies a personal spiritual intelligence embodied in the likeness of its own species and clothed upon with an outward tabernacle of eternal, incorruptible flesh and bones. This state of existence can only be attained by the resurrection of the body, and its eternal reunion with the spirit.

Eternal life thus attained, and endowed with the eternal attributes of intelligence and love, could never exercise, or derive enjoyment from the affections of the latter, unless associated with other beings endowed with the same attributes.

Hence the object, or necessity of eternal kindred ties, associations and affections, exercised as the attributes of that charity which never ends.

The third proposition, viz.—*Eternal peace,* could never be secured without the development of Eternal Law and government, which would possess in itself the attributes of infinite truth, goodness and power. Any government, short of this, could never guarantee *Eternal Peace.* It would be liable to be overthrown by the lack of truth to discern, disposition to execute, or power to enforce the measures necessary to insure peace.

The fourth proposition, viz.—*Eternal Wealth,* must, of necessity, consist of an everlasting inheritance or title, defined and secured by this eternal government, to portions of the organized elements, in their pure, incorruptible and eternal state.

In order to be wealthy, eternal man must possess a certain portion of the surface of some eternal planet, adapted to his order or sphere of existence.

This inheritance, incorruptible, eternal in the heavens, must be sufficiently extensive for his accommodation, with all his family dependencies. It must also comprise a variety of elements, adapted to his use and convenience. Eternal gold, silver, precious stones and other precious materials would be useful in the erection and furnishing of mansions and of public and private dwellings or edifices.

These edifices combined, or arranged in wisdom, would constitute eternal cities. Gardens, groves, walks, rivulets, fountains, flowers and fruits would beautify and adorn the landscape, please the eye, the taste, the smell, and thus contribute gladness to the heart of man.

Silks, linens, or other suitable materials would be necessary to adorn his person, and to furnish and beautify his mansions.

In short, eternal man in possession of eternal worlds, in all their variety and fullness, will eat, drink, think, converse, associate, assemble, disperse, go, come, possess, improve, love and enjoy. He will increase in riches, knowledge, power, might, majesty and dominion in worlds without end.

Every species of the animal creation ever organized by creative goodness, or that ever felt the pangs of death, or uttered a groan while subject to the king of terrors, or exulted in the joys of life and sympathy, and longed for the redemption of the body, will have part in the resurrection, and will live forever in their own spheres in the possession of peace, and a fullness of joy adapted to their several capacities.

O child of earth, conceived in corruption!
Brought forth in pain and sorrow! sojourning
In a world of mourning, mid sighs and tears,
And groans, and awaiting in sadness thy home
In the gloomy grave, as food for worms;
Lift up thy head, cast thine eyes around thee,
Behold yon countless hosts of shiny orbs,

Yon worlds of light and life. Then turn to earth,
Survey the solid globe, its mineral wealth,
Its gems, its precious stones, its gold, its springs;
Its gardens, forests, fruits and flowers;
Its countless myriads of breathing life,
From *Mote to Man,* through all the varied scale
of animated being.
Visit the gloomy caverns of the dead,
The ancient sepulchre, where e'en the worm
of death himself, has died for want of food,
And bones disjointed are crumbled fine, and
Mingled with the dust.
Nay, deeper still, descend the fathomless
Abyss of souls condemned, in darkness chained,
Or thrust in gloomy dungeons of despair—
Where the very names of Mercy, of Hope,
And of death's conqueror remain unknown.
Observe with care the whole, indulge in tears,
But hope, believe, and clothed with charity
Which never fails, thine eyes enlightened,
Thy person clad in light ethereal,
Time fades, and opens on eternity.
Again review the scene beheld before.
You startle, seem surprised! confused!, o'erwhelmed!
Death is conquered, corruption is no more,
All is *life,* and the word ETERNITY
Is inscribed in characters indelible
On every particle and form of life.

Socrates, Plato, Confucius, and many other philosophers and divines have written largely on the immortality of the *soul* or spirit of man.

Some of these have suffered, with joy and cheerfulness, imprisonment, torture, and even death, with only this limited view of eternal existence.

Could these martyrs to a portion of truth so limited, and yet so full of hope and consolation, have handled immortal flesh and bones in the persons of Enoch or Elijah translated, or of Jesus raised from the dead; could they have learned from their sacred lips, and realized the full import of that joyful sentence—

"Behold! I make all things new;"

could they have contemplated eternal worlds of matter in all its elements and forms of animal life, indissoluble and everlasting; could they have beheld eternal man, moving in the majesty of God, amid the planetary systems, grasping the knowledge of universal nature, and with an intellect enlightened by the experience and observations of thousands and even millions of years; could they have had a glimpse of all this, and heard the promise—

"There shall be no more death,"

issuing from the fountain of truth, prompted by infinite benevolence and charity, re-echoing amid the starry worlds, reaching down to earth, vibrating with a thrill of joy, all the myriads of animated nature, penetrating the gloomy vaults of death and the prisons of the spirit world, with a ray of hope, and causing to spring afresh, the well-springs of life, and joy and love, even in the lonely dungeons of despair! O! how would their bosoms have reverberated with unutterable joy and triumph, in view of changing worlds.

Could the rulers of this world have beheld, or even formed a conception of, such riches, such nobility, such an eternal and exceeding weight of glory, they would have accounted the wealth, pleasures, honors, titles, dignities, glories, thrones, principalities and crowns of this world as mere toys—the play-things of a day, dross, not worth the strife and toil of acquiring, or the trouble of maintaining, except as a duty or troublesome responsibility.

With this view of the subject, what man so base, so groveling, so blind to his own interests as to neglect those duties, self-denials, sacrifices which are necessary in order to secure a part in the First resurrection, and a far more exceeding and eternal weight of glory in that life which never ends?

CHAPTER EIGHT

Key of Knowledge, Power, and Government

Heaven's nobility, whom worlds obey,
Clad in the brightness of eternal day,
Enthroned in majesty, as *"Priests and Kings,"*
To whom the universe its incense brings!
Angels, its ministers! Heaven is its throne!
The stores of infinitude are all its own!

Having given a general view of the powers, operations, and effects of Theology, as developed amongst, the nations of antiquity, the mysteries of the Godhead, the law of nature, and the origin and destiny of the universe, the subject next in order is the Key of knowledge, power and government, as developed in the heavens and on the earth, for the organization, order, peace, happiness, education, improvement and exaltation of intelligences in the image of God—His sons and daughters.

The great family of man, comprising the inhabitants of unnumbered millions of worlds, in every variety and degree of progress, consists of five principal spheres or grand divisions in the scale of progressive being, viz.—

First. *The Gods,* composed of embodied spirits, who inhabit tabernacles of immortal flesh and bones in their most refined state, and who are perfected in all the attributes of intelligence and power.

Second. *The Angels,* who are also composed of spirits and immortal flesh and bones, less refined, and endowed with vast intelligence and power, but not a fullness.

Third. *Personal spirits,* without a tabernacle of flesh and bones. These are they who have passed the veil of death, and are awaiting a resurrection.

Fourth. *Personal spirits,* with mortal tabernacles, as in the present world.

Fifth. *Personal spirits,* who have not yet descended to be clothed upon with mortality, but who are candidates for the same.

There is also a sixth division, but of these we need not speak, as they are not, as yet, included in the scale of progressive being, not having kept their first estate.

The spirits of all men in their primeval states, were intelligent. But among these intelligences some were more noble, that is to say, more intelligent than others.

And God said, these will I make rulers. Upon this principle was manifested the election before the foundation of the world, of certain individuals to certain offices, as written in the Scriptures.

In other words, certain individuals, more intelligent than the others, were chosen by the Head, to teach, instruct, edify, improve, govern, and minister truth and salvation to others; and to hold the delegated powers or keys of government, in the several spheres of progressive being.

These were not only chosen, but set apart, by a holy ordinance in the eternal worlds, as embassadors, foreign ministers, priests, kings, apostles, etc., to fill the various stations in the vast empire of the Sovereign of all.

Jesus Christ, being the first Apostle thus commissioned, and the President of all the powers thus delegated, is Lord of lords, and King of kings, in the heavens and on the earth. Hence this Priesthood is called the Priesthood after the order of the Son of God. It holds the keys of all the true principles of government in all worlds, being without beginning of days or end of life. It was held by Adam, Seth, Enoch, Noah, Shem, Melchizedek and others. Abraham obtained this Priesthood, and an election of the same in his seed after him to all generations. The decree went forth in an everlasting covenant, that in Abraham and his seed all the nations and kindreds of the earth should be blessed.

Of this lineage according to the flesh were the Prophets, John the Baptist, Jesus Christ, and the Jewish Apostles. Since the covenant and election thus manifested, the keys of revelation, government and miraculous powers on earth have been held exclusively by the literal descendants of this noble and royal house.

The Gentiles could partake of a portion of the same blessings, but this could only be done through their ministry, and by adoption into the same family.

This election or covenant with the house of Israel will continue for ever. In the great restoration of all things, this lineage will hold the keys of Priesthood, salvation and government, for all nations. As saith the Prophet Isaiah—"*The nation and kingdom that will not serve thee shall perish; yea, those nations shall be utterly wasted.*"

And again—"*Ye shall be the priests of the Lord; men shall call you the ministers of our God: but strangers shall build your walls, and the sons of the alien shall be your ploughmen and your vine dressers.*"

This Priesthood, including that of the Aaronic, holds the keys of revelation of the oracles of God to man upon the earth; the power and right to give laws and commandments to individuals, churches, rulers, nations and the world; to appoint, ordain, and establish constitutions and kingdoms; to appoint kings, presidents, governors or judges, and to ordain or anoint them to their several holy callings, also to instruct, warn, or reprove them by the word of the Lord.

It also holds the keys of administration of ordinances for the remission of sins, and for the gift of the Holy Spirit; to heal the sick, cast out demons or work miracles in the name of the Lord; in fine, to bind or loose on earth and in heaven. For the exercise of all which powers the student of Theology will find abundant precedents in the sacred Scriptures.

Men holding the keys of the Priesthood and Apostleship after the order of the Son of God, are his representatives, or embassadors, to mankind. To receive them, to obey their instructions, to feed, clothe or aid them, is counted the same, in the final judgment, as if all had been done to the Son of God in person. On the other hand, to reject them or their testimony or message, or the word of God through them, in any matter, is counted the same as if done to Jesus Christ, in his own person. Indeed, such embassadors will be the final judges of the persons, rulers, cities or nations to whom they are sent.

Although the chosen instruments chosen to hold the keys of this Priesthood must be the literal lineage of Israel, yet that lineage are not all thus commissioned, nor indeed are any of them Priests merely because they are of the chosen seed. Such an instrument must be revealed, and his ordination, which he had before the world began, be renewed and confirmed upon his fleshly tabernacle, or he cannot be a Priest on earth.

One who already holds the authority, or keys of Priesthood, can reveal, by the word of the Lord, and ordain and anoint others to similar callings, and through these ordinances fill them with the Holy Spirit, as a qualification for their holy calling. By this means Joshua succeeded Moses, Elisha succeeded Elijah, etc. And by this means the great Apostle of the Father chose and ordained the Twelve Apostles of the Jews, and gave the keys or presidency of the Kingdom to Peter.

There have, however, been times when, by a general martyrdom or apostasy, the keys of this power have been taken from the earth (see chapters 2, 3, 4). In such case there would be no longer visions, revelations, or miraculous gifts from the Lord, manifested among men, because the Priesthood is the channel, and the ordinances are the means, through which such blessings are enjoyed by man. In the absence of these offices and powers, darkness, ignorance, superstition, priestcraft and kingcraft, idolatry, and every species of abuse would fill the earth, and usurp the place of the true government of the kingdom of God.

The most remarkable and long-continued instance of this kind, which perhaps ever transpired in our world, commenced with the destruction of the Apostles and Saints who immediately succeeded the Lord Jesus Christ, and continued until the present century, producing in its consequences all the human butcheries, wars, oppressions, misrule, ignorance, superstitions, kingcraft, priestcraft, and misery, which have visited the world in the false name of Christianity.

On the Western Hemisphere, the Apostleship, oracles, miracles and gifts of the Spirit, ceased from among the people in the fourth century.

The precise time of the discontinuance of these powers on the eastern continents, or in the Roman world, is not known. Suffice it to say, the last of the Twelve Apostles predicted, in his vision on the Isle of Patmos, the reign of a certain power which should make war with the Saints, overcome them, be drunken with their blood, and bear rule over all nations. "And by thy sorceries," said he, "were all nations deceived." If these predictions have had their fulfillment, then it is the height of inconsistency for any one to contend, that Rome or any nation has perpetuated the Priesthood, Apostleship, or Church. This would be the same as to say, the Saints were destroyed, and yet perpetuated; all nations were deceived, and yet had the truth.

Could a universal or catholic power at once destroy the Saints, and perpetuate them? Could the same power, at the same time, be the conservator and promulgator of a system of universal salvation and of universal deception?

But leaving the prediction, and the reasoning on this subject, what are the facts which present themselves for our inspection, clearly visible to all men?

Do we not find the world, for many ages, and up to the present time, destitute of those manifestations, visions, powers and keys of knowledge and government which would enlighten, purify, and exalt the race, and establish permanent righteousness and peace? In short, have the powers of the eternal Priesthood, as described and exemplified in the Holy Scriptures, and in this work, been manifested for the government of the Catholic, or Protestant world, or any nation thereof, since the destruction of the ancient Saints and Apostles?

If we answer this last question in the negative, then, we verify the truth of the prediction by the last of the Twelve; if in the affirmative, we deny both the truth of the prediction, and the facts which clearly present themselves in the past history and present circumstances of the world called "*Christian.*"

When there is no longer a commissioned Priesthood perpetuated on the earth, it becomes necessary in order to restore the government of God, for the man or men last holding the keys of such power to return to the earth as ministering angels, and to select, by the word of the Lord, and ordain, certain individuals of the royal lineage of Israel, to hold the keys of such Priesthood, and to ordain others, and thus restore and re-organize the government of God, or his Kingdom upon the earth.

After the destruction of the Apostles and Saints, who succeeded Jesus Christ, there is but one dispensation or restoration predicted by the Prophets.

That dispensation will fulfill the times of the Gentiles, complete their fullness, restore the kingdom to Israel, gather home their twelve tribes, organize them into a theocratic government, that is, a government founded and guided by Prophets, Priesthood, visions and revelations. It will, in fact, not only restore to them the ministration of angels, but receive its final consummation by the resurrection of the ancient Saints, and their return to the earth, accompanied by the Son of God in his own proper person. To this dispensation all nations must submit.

All merely human religious or political institutions, all republics, states, kingdoms, empires, must be dissolved, the dross of ignorance and falsehood be separated, and the golden principles of unalloyed truth be preserved, and blended for ever in the one consolidated, universal, eternal government of the Saints of the Most High, and all nations shall serve and obey Him.

See Book of Abraham, translated from papyrus, taken from the Catacombs of Thebes in Egypt, contained in the Pearl of Great Price (Abr. 3:23).

CHAPTER NINE

Revival or Restoration of the Science of Theology in the Present Age

A modern Prophet! Yes, a mighty Seer!
From Israel's royal line, must next appear;
Clad in the spirit of Elijah's power,
To prune the vineyard in th' eleventh hour;
To light the dawn of that effulgent day,
When King Messiah shall his sceptre sway.

The nineteenth century opened upon the world with far more favorable auspices than any other age since the destruction of the people of the Saints, and the reign of universal mystery. That spirit of freedom, and independence of thought, of speech, and of action, which a few centuries before had germinated in Europe, and which, after a stunted growth amid the thorns and thistles of kingcraft, the tares of priestcraft, and the weeds of superstition, in the old world, transplanted itself and obtained a more vigorous growth in the new world, had now grown to a degree of maturity, and become consolidated, opening resources for all nations, under the inestimable guarantee of constitutional liberty.

To this standard the most enterprising, intelligent and thinking of every nation in Europe had commenced to gather like a flowing stream, Here, far separated from the practical influence, the false glare, the empty show, or even the senseless name and titles of a self-styled or imaginary nobility, their minds enlarged, their energies had full scope, and their intellectual faculties, unfettered and free, and surrounded with inexhaustible stores of unoccupied elementary riches, soon opened and developed new channels of thought, of action, of enterprise and improvement, the results of which have revolutionized the world in regard to geographical knowledge, commerce, intercommunication, transportation, travel, transmission of news, and mutual acquaintance and interchange of thought.

The triumphs of steam over earth and sea, the extension of railroads, and, above all, the lightning powers of telegraph, are already, gradually but rapidly, developing, concentrating and consolidating the energies and interests of all nations, preparatory to the universal development of knowledge, neighborly kindness and mutual brotherhood.

Physically speaking, there seems to need but the consummation of two great enterprises more, in order to complete the preparations necessary for the fulfillment of Isaiah and other Prophets, in regard to the restoration of Israel to Palestine, from the four quarters of the earth, and the annual re-union of all nations to the new standards, holy shrines and temples of Zion and Jerusalem, under the auspices of that great, universal and permanent theocracy which is to succeed the long reign of mystery.

These things achieved, even the most incredulous in regard to the truth of Scripture prophecy will be constrained to acknowledge that, physically and politically speaking, there is nothing impossible, or even improbable in the belief, that the twelve tribes of Israel will be concentrated from all nations in their own land, that Jerusalem will become the capital of political government, the seat of knowledge, and the shrine of worship for the yearly resort of all the nations and countries included in the world known to the Prophets of old; while the Western Hemisphere, separated, as it is, by two great oceans from the Old World, will naturally form its own central capital, its Zion, or New Jerusalem, to which all tribes and nations may perform their annual visits for instruction, devotion and mutual interchange of thought, of fellowship and affection.

Can the student of prophecy contemplate all these preparations, clearly predicted thousands of years ago, and now bursting upon the world with seemingly preconcerted connection and exactness, revolutionizing all things in a single age, and not be struck with the reflection that the hand of God must be in all this, and that moral energy and spiritual light must be forthcoming from the heavens commensurate with the physical and political preparations for a new era?

The same Prophets who have contemplated and described the development of national freedom, universal intercourse, mutual peace, knowledge, union of worship, reunion of the tribes of Israel; who have described highways, trains of cars flying as it were with a cloud, ocean steamers, ships, litters and swift beasts as the instruments of restoration, have also predicted that, in connection with all these preparations, a new dispensation should be manifested, a new covenant established, "a standard" for the nations, "an ensign" for the people. In short, "swift messengers," "teachers," prophets would be commissioned, revelations be manifested, and a new organization be developed, fitted to the times, and with the principles and laws adapted to the reorganization, order, and government of a renovated world.

Where and when should we look for the "grain of mustard seed," the germ, the nucleus of such organization? of course, in a land of free institutions, where such organizations could be legally developed and claim constitutional protection, until sufficiently matured to defend itself against the convulsions, the death struggles, the agonizing throes, which precede the dissolution of the long reign of mystic tyranny: and at a time when modern freedom had been consolidated, nationalized, and its standard recognized among the nations.

Such an organization should also be looked for, in its first development, as contemporary with the first dawn or development of the physical and political means provided for the same result.

The beginning of the present century gave birth to those chosen instruments who were destined to hold the keys of restoration for the renovation of the world.

The United States of America was the favored nation raised up, with institutions adapted to the protection and free development of the necessary truths, and their practical results. And that great Prophet, Apostle and martyr—

JOSEPH SMITH,

was the Elias, the Restorer, the presiding messenger, holding the keys of the *"Dispensation of the fulness of times."*

Yes, that extraordinary man, whose innocent blood is now dripping, as it were, from the hands of assassins and their accessories, in the United States, was the chosen vessel honored of God, and ordained by angels, to ordain other Apostles and Elders, to restore the Church and Kingdom of God, the gifts of the Holy Spirit, and to be a messenger in the spirit and power of Elijah, to prepare the way of the Lord. "For, behold, he will suddenly come to his temple!"

Like John, who filled a similar mission preparatory to the first advent of the Son of God, he baptized with water unto repentance, for the remission of sins; like him, he was imprisoned; and, like him, his life was taken from the earth; and, finally, like all other, true messengers, his message is being demonstrated by its progressive fulfillment—the powers, gifts, and signs following the administration of his message in all the world, and every minute particular of his predictions fulfilling in the order of events, as the wheels of time bring them due.

But in one important point his message differs from all former messages. The science of Theology revived by him will never decline, nor its keys be taken from the earth. They are committed to man for the last time. Their consummation will restore the tribes of Israel and Judah; overthrow all corrupt institutions; usher in the reign of universal peace and knowledge, introduce to earth her lawful and eternal King, the crucified Nazarene, the resurrected Messiah, banish darkness and death, sorrow, mourning and tears, from the face of our globe; and crown our race with the laurels of victory and eternal life.

Ages yet unborn will rise up and call him blessed. A thousand generations of countless myriads will laud his name and recount his deeds, while unnumbered nations bask in the light and enjoy the benefits of the institution founded by his instrumentality.

His kindred, the nation that gave him birth, and exulted at his death, nay, his very murderers and their posterity, will yet come bending unto him, and seek his forgiveness, and the benefits of his labors.

But, oh! the pain! the dark despair! the torments of a guilty conscience! the blackness of darkness in the lower hell, which the guilty wretches will experience before that happy day of deliverance!

Oh! the countless myriads of the offspring of innocent and honorable men who will walk the earth, tread on the ashes, or plow and reap over the bones and dust of those miserable murderers and their accomplices who have consented to the shedding of innocent blood, ere the final trump shall sound, which calls up their sleeping dust from its long slumbers in the tomb, and their spirits from the prison of the damned.

And even when this, to them almost interminable, period has rolled away, and they rise from the dead, instead of a welcome exaltation to the presence and society of the sons of God, an eternal banishment awaits them. They never can come where God and Christ dwell, but will be servants in the dominions of the Saints, their former victims.

This extraordinary personage was born in Sharon, Windsor County, Vermont, United States, December 23rd, 1805.

He removed with his father, during childhood, and settled near Palmyra, in Wayne County, New York. Amid these forest wilds he was reared a farmer, and inured to all the hardships, toils, and privations of a newly settled country. His education was therefore very limited. When about seventeen years of age, he had several open visions, in which a holy angel ministered to him, admonished him for his sins, taught him repentance, and faith in the crucified and risen Messiah, opened to him the Scriptures of the Prophets, unfolding the field of prophecy pertaining to the latter-day glory, and the doctrines of Christ and his ancient Apostles.

On the 22nd of September, 1827, the angel directed him to a hill a few miles distant, called anciently Cumorah. Around this hill, in the fifth century of the Christian era, had rallied the last remnant of a once powerful and highly polished nation called the Nephites.

Here, two hundred and thirty thousand men, women and children marshaled themselves for a last, defense, in legions of ten thousand each, under their respective commanders, at whose head was the renowned Mormon, the general of a hundred battles. And here they received the enemy in untold numbers, and melted away before them, till none remained, except a few that fled to the southward, and a few that fell wounded, and were left by the enemy among the unburied dead.

Among these latter were General Mormon, and his son, and second in command—General Moroni.

These were the last Prophets of a nation, now no more. They held the sacred records, compiled and transmitted from their fathers, from the remotest antiquity. They held the Urim and Thummim, and the compass of Lehi, which had been prepared by Providence, to guide a colony from Jerusalem to America.

In the Hill Cumorah, they deposited all these things. Here they lay concealed for fourteen hundred years. And here did the angel Moroni direct the young Joseph to behold these sacred things, in their sacred deposit, and to receive, from these long-silent and gloomy archives, an abridged record of the whole, and with it the Urim and Thummim.

The abridged record, thus obtained, was engraved in Egyptian characters, on gold plates, by the hands of the two Prophets and Generals—Mormon and Moroni. By the instructions of the angel, and the use of the Urim and Thummim, the youthful Joseph, now a Prophet and Seer, was enabled to translate the abridgment, or rather the unsealed portion which was destined for the present age.

This done, the angel of the Lord appeared to three other persons, called Martin Harris, Oliver Cowdery, and David Whitmer; showed them the golden plates, and the engravings thereon; bore testimony of there correct translation by the Prophet Joseph, and commanded them to bear a faithful testimony of the same. Two of these were respectable farmers, and the other was a school-master.

Early in 1830, this translation, with the accompanying testimony, was published in English, in the United States, under the title of the Book of Mormon.

It is now 1853 translated and published in nearly all European languages.

This book more deeply interests the world, and every intelligent, accountable being therein, than any other book, save the Jewish Scriptures, which is now extant. Its history penetrates the otherwise dark oblivion of the past, as it regards America, through the remote ages of antiquity; follows up the stream of the generations of man, till arriving at the great fountain, the distributor of nations, tribes and tongues—the Tower of Babel, it ceases, or is lost in, and sweetly blended with, that one great undivided Adamic river, whose source is in Paradise, the cradle of man, whose springs issue from beneath the throne of the Eternal; and whose secret fountains comprise the infinite expanse, the boundless ocean of intellect, fact and historic truth, as recorded in the archives of eternity. Its prophetic vision opens the events of unborn time. The fate of nations; the restoration of Judah and Israel; the downfall of corrupt churches and institutions; the end of superstition and misrule; the universal prevalence of peace, truth, light and knowledge; the awful wars which precede those happy times; the glorious coming of Jesus Christ as King; the resurrection of the Saints, to reign upon the earth; the great, grand rest of a thousand years; the jubilee of universal nature upon our planet, are all predicted in that book. The time and means of their fulfillment are pointed out with clearness, showing the present age more pregnant with events than all the ages of Adam's race which have gone before it. Its doctrines are developed in such plainness and simplicity, and with such clearness and precision, that no man can mistake them. They are there as they flowed from the mouth of a risen Redeemer, in the liquid eloquence of love, mingled with immortal tears of joy and compassion and were written by men whose tears of overwhelming affection and gratitude bathed his immortal feet.

It was ascertained by revelation, by means of the Urim and Thummim, that the youthful Prophet Joseph was of the house of Israel, of the tribe of Joseph.

He continued to receive visions, revelations, and the ministry of angels, by whom he was at length ordained to the Apostleship, or High Priesthood after the order of Melchizedek, to hold the keys of the kingdom of God, the dispensation of the fullness of times.

Thus qualified, he proceeded, on the 6th of April, A.D. 1830, to organize the Church of the Saints, which then consisted of six members. The gifts of healing, of prophecy, of visions and miracles, began to be manifested among the believers, thus confirming his testimony with signs following.

In this same year, the principles restored by him were proclaimed, and branches of the Church were organized in various parts of his own state, in Pennsylvania, Ohio, and elsewhere; and the number of his disciples increased from six members to upwards of one thousand.

During the three following years, hundreds of ministers, ordained by him, were sent out in all directions through the country, and branches of the Church were organized in most of the states of the American Union.

In 1835, he ordained, by commandment of the Lord a quorum of Twelve Apostles, and several quorums of Seventy, as a traveling ministry.

In 1836, a temple was completed and dedicated, in Kirtland, Ohio; in which these quorums, and the Priesthood in general were assembled in a school of Prophets, and were instructed, and anointed to their holy calling. In this same year, some of the Apostles visited Upper Canada, and spread the fullness of the Gospel in Toronto and all the region round, gathering several branches of the Church.

In 1837, a mission was sent to England, which was attended with the same powers, and with remarkable success.

In 1838, the state of Missouri undertook the extermination of the Church from its borders, murdered many men, women and children, and finally succeeded in the forcible expulsion of about ten thousand people, and the seizure of their lands and property.

In 1840, the quorum of the Twelve Apostles visited England, gathered great numbers into the Church, and published the Book of Mormon and several other works, among which was a periodical called the *Millennial*

Star, which now, in 1853, has a circulation of nearly eighteen thousand copies weekly.

Between the years, 1840 and 1844, our youthful Prophet gathered about him many thousands of his disciples; erected the great city of Nauvoo, on the banks of the Mississippi, commenced the erection of one of the most splendid temples in the world; and organized a legion of citizen soldiers for its defense. This Legion comprised nearly six thousand men, and was commanded by the young Prophet Joseph, who held a government commission, as Lieutenant-General.

From this center of science and heavenly light, there emanated rays, by the aid of foreign ministry, penetrating afar, lighted up the dawn of that effulgent day which is destined to break over all the earth, and shine forever.

Apostles, High Priests, Elders, Counselors and ministers of every degree, here thronged our youthful Prophet and hero, and were taught in this great school of Theology and spiritual philosophy; while a hundred thousand disciples in the nation and beyond the seas, looked to this centre for light and instruction.

Such was the progress of the science of Theology, revived in the present age; such the result of fourteen years of the ministry of an unlettered youth, crying in the wilderness the proclamation of repentance, baptizing for the remission of sins, and holding the keys of this divine, eternal power.

His unparalleled success, and still increasing influence, now alarmed his former persecutors, and raised their jealousy and envy to the highest pitch of frenzy and madness.

Several counties of Illinois combined with the former enemies, who had robbed and destroyed the Saints of Missouri, and, calling public meetings, passed resolutions to destroy the city of Nauvoo, and to force the Saints, once more to abandon their homes and farms to the possession of the land pirates. They also entered into covenant, to take the life of the young Joseph.

To resist this overwhelming storm, our hero and Prophet marshaled his legion of six thousand men, in his beloved city of Nauvoo, prepared for the most vigorous defense, and awaited the onset. The cowardly enemy soon discovered the impropriety of an open attack, and resolved on stratagem. They caused a magistrate of their own number to issue a writ; and sent a constable to bring the person of Joseph into the midst of those who had sworn to kill him. To yield to this mockery would be to lose his life. To resist it would be construed into treason and would bring on him the whole forces of the state. This stratagem succeeded—Nauvoo, its legion and its general were declared in rebellion. His Excellency, Thomas Ford, Governor of the state of Illinois, mustered an army, marched to the scene of conflict, took sides with the enemy, and in fact incorporated their entire forces with his own troops.

With this formidable force he marched to Carthage, a small town eighteen miles from Nauvoo. He then sent a captain named, Singleton to take command of the Nauvoo Legion, and demanded its Lieutenant-General to repair to Carthage, and place himself in the hands of those who had publicly combined to take his life. Sooner than have submitted to these insults and humiliating demands, the Legion would have joyfully marched to Carthage, and cut to pieces this cowardly band of rebels against American institutions and all the rights of man.

But the Saints were located between two powerful states, who were now combined against the laws, constitutions and liberties of their country. To destroy one army, or even resist its most extravagant demands, would be to draw upon themselves and families, the overwhelming forces of the ferocious, ignorant, and worse than savage beings who had long thirsted for their plunder and their blood.

The young Prophet had no confidence in the Governor's pledge to protect his person. He felt the hour had come, when his own blood alone could appease the enemy, and preserve the lives of his flock. He restrained the ardor of the Legion; called upon them, by the love they had ever borne to him as a Prophet and Apostle; and conjured them, by the respect and confidence they had shown him as their General, to submit to the extravagant demands of his Excellency, and leave the event with God. He now took an affectionate leave of his beloved legion, who were dissolved in tears; tore himself from the embrace of his aged and widowed mother, and frantic wife and children, and repaired to Carthage. He was accompanied by his brother Hyrum, and the two of the Twelve that were not abroad on foreign missions, who would not forsake him. On the way he was cheerful, but solemn. He spoke little, but observed to those about him: "*I am going like a lamb to the slaughter; but I am calm as a summer's morning; I have a conscience void of offense towards God, and towards all men, I shall die innocent; and it shall yet be said of me—He was murdered in cold blood.*"

Arriving at Carthage, he delivered himself to his enemies; answered to the charge of the original writ, to enforce which all the Governor's forces had been mustered, and was then committed to prison to answer the charge of treason.

In this dungeon he was still accompanied by the two Apostles and his brother Hyrum, who were determined to die with him.

Here, as the four friends sat in the upper room, singing hymns, on the afternoon of the 27th day of June, 1844, the prison was suddenly surrounded with demons in the flesh, armed with muskets and bayonets, and their faces as black as Cain—the original murderer. These commenced firing through the doors and windows of the prison, while a portion assaulted and broke open the door. Hyrum suddenly fell, and died without a groan, being pierced with four balls. Taylor fled, wounded and bleeding, to the window, and was about to throw himself out, when a ball aimed at his heart hit his watch in his vest pocket, and threw him back into the room. The other Apostle, Willard Richards, stood and parried the guns with his hand staff, receiving slight injury.

In the midst of all this scene, the Prophet's presence of mind did not forsake him. He saw his brother Hyrum fall, stiffen and die. He then exclaimed, in the anguish of his soul—"O my brother!" and sprang for the window, amid showers of ball as thick as hail. He instantly threw himself from the upper story into the midst of the bristling bayonets of the enemy, and, on alighting, was pierced with a shower of balls and instantly died without a struggle or a groan.

His presence of mind and prompt action in thus throwing himself among the enemy, drew them from the prison in time to save the lives of the two Apostles, which was, no doubt, the object of this, the last glorious act of his life.

Thus ended the mortal career of a youth who had revealed the ancient history of a continent; restored to man the keys and powers of the divine science of Theology; organized the Church and Kingdom of God, and revealed and re-established those principles, which will eventually prevail, and govern the sons of earth in countless ages yet unborn. "The good shepherd," said Jesus, "layeth down his life for the sheep."

When the news of this horrid tragedy spread abroad, the fear of vengeance from the Nauvoo Legion seized the Governor, his troops, and the whole gang of pirates; all fled, and even the inhabitants of the guilty villages in the vicinity vacated their habitations, and fled in terror and dismay.

As the news reached Nauvoo, a thrill of horror and of anguish unutterable ran, as with electricity, through every pulse. The Legion sprang to arms, and would have desolated the whole rebel counties, now left unprotected, had not their judgments balanced the burning attribute of justice which swelled their bosoms.

As it was, they smothered their resentment, and prepared for the burial of the illustrious dead. The bodies of the two martyrs were borne to the city, being met by the entire populace, bowed with sorrow, bathed in tears, and their bosoms unheaved with a sense of sorrow and outraged humanity, such as, perhaps an entire populace at once never felt, since man was doomed to mourn.

The Twelve, who were abroad soon returned, soothed and comforted the sheep, and exhorted them to union and perseverance. The work on the Temple was resumed, and finally completed, at an expense of many hundred thousand dollars. In this holy edifice, after its dedication to the Lord, a portion of the Priesthood received those holy washings, anointings, keys, ordinances, oracles and instructions which were yet wanting to perfect them in the fullness of the Priesthood.

In the autumn of 1845, the enemy again rallied, and commenced to desolate the borders of the Nauvoo settlements by fire and sword.

Wearied with long-continued vexation and persecution, the council of the Apostles now determined to seek peace for the Saints amid the far-off and almost unexplored deserts and mountains of the interior.

In February, 1846, this emigration was commenced, headed by the Apostles and their families.

On the 24th of July, 1847, the first pioneers of this vast emigration, headed by the President of the whole Church, Brigham Young, entered the valley of Great Salt Lake.

In the meantime, the beautiful Nauvoo, and its surrounding farms and villas fell a prey to the enemy, after a vigorous defense. Its Temple, the pride and glory of America, was laid in ashes. Its last remnant plundered, robbed of their all, sick, destitute, wounded, bleeding, dying, at length disappeared beyond the horizon of the illimitable plains of the west, and for a moment, the curtain of oblivion closed over this strange drama, and the Kingdom of God seemed lost to mortal view.

Again it rises, and what do we behold!

The banner of freedom unfurled a thousand miles from the frontiers of the persecuting foe; its waving folds, amid the snow-clad peaks of the

Rocky Mountains, inviting to liberty and light, the oppressed of every clime; and a free and sovereign State rising, in majesty and smiling splendor, amid the fastnesses of nature's eternal ramparts; while the exhaustless treasures of the golden mountains of California, revealed by the providence-guiding keys of modern Theology, are poured like a flowing stream into the treasury of the Lord, to aid in the gathering and subsistence of the Saints.

Can the student of Theology contemplate all these grand events and their results, all verging to one focus, all combining to prepare the way for the consummation of the entire volume of unfulfilled prophecy, and still be so much at a loss as to query, like one of old: "Art thou he that should come; or, look we for another?" If so, we can only recommend, to one so slow of heart, to search the Scriptures, and all good books extant on the subject. And, while he searches, let him turn from his sins, and live in newness of life, and call upon God, the Father of all, in the name of Messiah, that his understanding may be enlightened, and his stubborn heart subdued and constrained to yield to the force of Truth.

CHAPTER TEN

Keys of Initiation in Practical Theology

Is't possible! A sinful man like me,
A candidate for heaven's mystery!
May I approach the gate and enter in,
Be wash'd and cleans'd from all my former sin,
Renew'd in spirit, and partake the power
of bless'd Theology from this good hour.

The student of this deeply interesting science, who has traced with us the thrilling incidents of its history on earth, till he finds it restored in all its beauties, and its powers taking root in the earth, to bear eternal fruit, will, doubtless, feel a desire to be instructed in the first principles—the ordinances or means by which he may personally partake of its benefits, and exercise its gifts.

There are certain qualifications, or personal preparations indispensably necessary, without which, no person can be a proper candidate for blessings so divine.

First. He must believe in Jesus Christ, and in the testimony of the Apostle, or commissioned officer, to whom he looks for the administration of these blessings.

Secondly. He must forsake a sinful course of life; must deny himself every impure or unlawful indulgence; must do right with his fellow creatures, and determine to keep the commandments of Jesus Christ.

With these qualifications he comes to the Apostle, Elder, or Priest of the Church of the Saints, who, after a covenant on the part of the candidate to forsake his sins, and keep the commandments of Jesus Christ, goes down into the water with him, and there buries him, in the name of the Father, Son and Holy Spirit, for remission of sins, and then raises him from his watery grave.

This ordinance is to represent the death, burial and resurrection of Jesus Christ, and is called Baptism.

Having passed through this ordinance, the hands of some one, or more, of the authorized Priesthood, are next laid upon the head of the candidate, in the same sacred names, and the gift of the Holy Spirit is confirmed upon him. This baptism of water and of the Spirit is called a new birth: and it is in reality a repetition of the natural birth, or entrance into the elements of a new existence.

To realize this, the student must be indoctrinated in the philosophy of this natural birth, which involves three principles, viz.—"*The spirit, the water and the blood.*"

The embryo formation of the human body, is commenced and sustained by blood and spirit, in the womb of nature, where, until the period of birth, it floats in the element of water. At birth, then, it is literally born of water, that is, it emerges from that element in which it has been so long immersed, into a different element, called the atmosphere, which then becomes a necessary element of existence.

To be born again, then, is to enter into the same element, suspend the breath in the watery womb, and emerge from that element into the atmosphere, and again gasp the first breath in the new creation; while, at the same time, the blood of atonement is applied to the individual, for remission of sins, and is followed by the outpouring of the Holy Spirit of promise. As it is written,—"*There are three that bear record on the earth; the spirit, the water, and the blood.*"

The things of this visible creation, are the patterns of things in the invisible world; and are so arranged as to exactly correspond—the one answering to the other, as face to face in a mirror.

The immersion in water, in the name of the Father, Son, and Holy Spirit, for remission of sins; and the baptism of the Holy Spirit, which follows according to promise, by the laying on of hands of the holy Priesthood; were instituted from before the foundation of the world, as a pattern of the birth, death, resurrection and new life of man.

The candidate is now initiated into the first principles of the science of Divine Theology. His mind is quickened, his intellectual faculties are aroused to intense activity. He is, as it were, illuminated. He learns more of divine truth in a few days, than he could have learned in a life time in the best merely human institutions in the world.

His affections are also purified, exalted, and increased in proportion. He loves his heavenly Father, and Jesus Christ, with a perfect love. He also loves the members of the Church, or the body of Christ, as he loves his own soul; while his bosom swells with the tenderest sympathies, and emotions of good will and benevolence, for all mankind. He would make any sacrifice which might be expedient, to do good. He would lay down his life most cheerfully, without one moment's hesitation or regret, if required of him by the cause of truth.

He also feels the spirit of prayer and watchfulness continually, and pours out his soul in the same, and finds he is answered in all things which are expedient. He is now in a fit capacity to exercise some one or more of the spiritual gifts.

He may perhaps speak in power, in the word of wisdom, in the word of knowledge, in prophecy, or in other tongues. He may see a vision, dream an inspired dream, or possess the gift to be healed, or to heal others, by the laying on of hands in the name of Jesus Christ.

To impart a portion of the Holy Spirit by the touch, or by the laying on of hands; or to impart a portion of the element of life, from one animal body to another, by an authorized agent who acts in the name of God, and who is filled therewith, is as much in accordance with the laws of nature, as for water to seek its own level; air its equilibrium, or heat, and electricity their own mediums of conveyance.

This law of spiritual fluid, its communicative properties, and the channel by which it is imparted from one person to another, bear some resemblance, or analogy, to the laws and operations of electricity. Like electricity, it is imparted by the contact of two bodies, through the channel of the nerves.

But the two fluids differ very widely. The one is a property nearly allied to the grosser elements of matter; not extensively endowed with the attributes of intelligence, wisdom, affection or moral discrimination. It can therefore be imparted from one animal body to another, irrespective of the intellectual or moral qualities of the subject or recipient. The other is a substance endowed with the attributes of intelligence, affection, moral discrimination, love, charity, and benevolence pure as the emotions which swell the bosom, thrill the nerves, or vibrate the pulse of the Father of all.

An agent filled with this heavenly fluid cannot impart of the same to another, unless that other is justified, washed, cleansed from all his impurities of heart, affections, habits or practices, by the blood of atonement, which is generally applied in connection with the baptism of remission.

A man who continues in his sins, and who has no living faith in the Son of God, cannot receive the gift of the Holy Spirit through the ministration of any agent, however holy he may be. The impure spirit of such a one will repulse the pure element, upon the natural laws of sympathetic affinity, or of attraction and repulsion.

An intelligent being, in the image of God, possesses every organ, attribute, sense, sympathy, affection, of will, wisdom, love, power and gift, which is possessed by God himself.

But these are possessed by man, in his rudimental state, in a subordinate sense of the word. Or, in other words, these attributes are in embryo; and are to be gradually developed. They resemble a bud—a germ, which gradually develops into bloom, and then, by progress, produces the mature fruit, after its own kind.

The gift of the Holy Spirit adapts itself to all these organs or attributes. It quickens all the intellectual faculties, increases, enlarges, expands and purifies all the natural passions and affections; and adapts them, by the gift of wisdom, to their lawful use. It inspires, develops, cultivates and matures all the fine-toned sympathies, joys, tastes, kindred feelings and affections of our nature. It inspires virtue, kindness, goodness, tenderness, gentleness and charity. It develops beauty of person, form and features. It tends to health, vigor, animation and social feeling. It develops and invigorates all the faculties of the physical and intellectual man. It strengthens, invigorates, and gives tone to the nerves. In short, it is, as it were, marrow to the bone, joy to the heart, light to the eyes, music to the ears, and life to the whole being.

In the presence of such persons, one feels to enjoy the light of their countenances, as the genial rays of a sunbeam. Their very atmosphere diffuses a thrill, a warm glow of pure gladness and sympathy, to the heart and nerves of others who have kindred feelings, or sympathy of spirit. No matter if the parties are strangers, entirely unknown to each other in person or character; no matter if they have never spoken to each other, each will be apt to remark in his own mind, and perhaps exclaim, when referring to the interview—"O what an atmosphere encircles that stranger! How my heart thrilled with pure and holy feelings in his presence! What confidence and sympathy he inspired! his countenance and spirit gave me more assurance, than a thousand written recommendations, or introductory letters." Such is the gift of the Holy Spirit, and such are its operations, when received through the lawful channel—the divine, eternal Priesthood.

CHAPTER ELEVEN

Philosophy of Miracles

Trembling with awe and fear, the mind inquires—
"What master spirit, now, the bard inspires;
What bold philosophy shall dare assign
A law to govern miracles divine—
Tell how effects transpire without a cause,
And how kind nature breaks kind nature's laws?"

Among the popular errors of modern times, an opinion prevails that miracles are events which transpire contrary to the laws of nature, that they are effects without a cause.

If such is the fact, then, there never has been a miracle, and there never will be one. The laws of nature are the laws of *truth*. Truth is unchangeable, and independent in its own sphere.

That which, at first sight, appears to be contrary to the known laws of nature, will always be found, on investigation, to be in perfect accordance with those laws. For instance, had a sailor of the last century been running before the wind, and met with a vessel running at a good rate of speed, directly in opposition to the wind and current, this sight would have presented, to his understanding, a miracle in the highest possible sense of the term, that is, an event entirely contrary to the laws of nature as known to him. Or if a train of cars, loaded with hundreds of passengers or scores of tons of freight had been seen passing over the surface of the earth, at the rate of sixty miles per hour, and propelled seemingly, by its own inherent powers of locomotion, our fathers would have beheld a miracle—an event which would have appeared, to them to break those very laws of nature with which they were the most familiar.

If the last generation had witnessed the conveyance of news from London to Paris, in an instant, while they knew nothing of the late invention of the electric telegraph, they would have testified, in all candor, and with the utmost assurance, that a miracle had been performed, in open violation of the well known laws of nature, and contrary to all human knowledge of cause and effect.

But, once familiar with the arts of the living age, all those miracles cease to be such, and the laws of nature, and of cause and effect, are found to be still moving, unimpaired, in all the harmony of primeval existence and operation.

The same views will apply with equal force to all the spiritual phenomena of the universe.

The terms *miracle* and *mystery* must become obsolete, and finally disappear from the vocabulary of intelligences, as they advance in the higher spheres of intellectual consistency. Even now they should be used only in a relative or limited sense, as applicable to those things which are not yet within reach of our powers or means of comprehension.

We will here remind the student of two principles, or laws of existence, developed in a former chapter of this work, which will account for all the miraculous powers of the universe—all the mighty works ever manifested by God, or by his servants.

First. All the elements of the material universe are eternal.

Second. There is a divine substance, fluid or essence, called Spirit, widely diffused among these eternal elements.

This spiritual substance is the most refined, subtle and powerful element in the universe. It is endowed with all wisdom, all knowledge, all intelligence and power. In short, it is the light, life, power and principle of all things, by which they move; and of all intelligences, by which they think.

This divine element, or Spirit, is the immediate, active or controlling agent, in all holy, miraculous powers.

Angels, and all holy men, perform all their miracles, simply, to use a modern magnetic term, by being in *"communication"* with this divine substance. Two beings, or two millions—any number, thus placed in *"communication"*—all possess one mind. The mind of the one is the mind of the other, the will of the one is the will of the other, the word of the one is the word of the other. And the holy fluid, or Spirit, being in communication with them all, goes forth to control the elements, and to execute all their mandates which are legally issued, in accordance with the mind and wisdom of the Great Eloheim.

God the Father is the Head. The mandates of Jesus Christ must be in the name of the Father.

The mandates of angels, or of holy men, in order to be legal, or of due force and power, must be issued in the name of Jesus Christ, or of the three who compose the Head Council; and must be in accordance with their united mind and will. The Holy Spirit then goes forth and executes their mandates. This agency being *invisible* and the effect *visible,* the act performed appears to those who are unacquainted with spiritual agency, as a miracle, or an *effect* without a *cause.*

When Jesus Christ was clothed upon with a mortal tabernacle, He had not the fullness of this divine substance at the first, but grew and increased in the same, till, being raised from the dead, He received a fullness and, therefore, had all power, in heaven and on earth.

His Apostles received a portion of this Spirit, but not a fullness, while they were mortal; therefore, they could know and perform some things, but not all.

The members of the Church also partook of this Spirit, through the ministry of the Apostles, by which miraculous gifts were imparted unto them, some to one and some to another: some to speak in tongues, some to interpret, or translate from one language into another; some to prophesy, see visions, or converse with angels; others to control, or cast out devils, or heal the sick; and others, again, to teach and edify the Church, or the world, by the word of wisdom, and by the word of knowledge.

All these gifts and miracles were the workings of that one, and the self-same Spirit given to the members of the Church of the Saints, while the world did not partake of a sufficient measure of the Spirit to possess these gifts. The reason of this is that they did not repent, and believe in Jesus Christ, and be baptized in his name, and receive the gift of the Holy Spirit, by the laying on of the hands of the Priesthood—these duties and ordinances being the legal or appointed channel by which the gift of the Holy Spirit was imparted. The reason why these gifts of the Spirit have not been enjoyed in all ages of the so-called *"Christian church"* is because it is not the true Church; nor, is the true ministry or Apostleship to be found among the Church, or Churches, where these gifts are denied.

Every minister and member of such institutions have need to repent, and be baptized, in the name of Jesus Christ, for remission of sins; and to receive the gift of the Holy Spirit, by the laying on of hands of those who have authority, in order to enter into the Kingdom of God.

These ordinances, ministered by a legal Priesthood, being divinely appointed, are the only legitimate means by which man may receive and exercise these divine powers; or, in other words, they are the means ordained of God, by which one being may communicate or impart a portion of this divine substance to another, so as to place that other in communication with the Father, Son, and Holy Spirit, and with angels, and the spirits of just men in the world of spirits, and with the members of the true Church on the earth.

To heal a person by the touch, or by the laying on of hands, in the name of Jesus Christ, or to impart the Holy Spirit by the laying on of hands, is as much in accordance with the laws of nature, as for water to seek its own level, an apple to fall to the ground when loosened from the tree where it grew, quicksilver to attract its own affinities.

A person commissioned of Jesus Christ, and filled with this spiritual substance, can impart of the same to another, provided there is a preparation of heart, and faith on the part of the receiver. Or if, as in cases of healing, casting out devils, etc., it happens that the receiver has no command of his own mind—as in cases of little children, persons swooned, fainted, deranged or dead, then the *faith* of the administrator alone, or in connection with other friends and agents, in his behalf, is sufficient in many cases to perform the work.

However, the touch, or laying on of hands, is not the only means of communicating the gift of healing. A word spoken, a mandate issued, or even a handkerchief, apron, or other garment, worn or touched by a person full of this Spirit, and conveyed to another, has, according to sacred history, and also the experience of the present age, proved sufficient to communicate the spiritual fluid, between minds of strong and mutual faith. So well acquainted was the Prophet Elisha with this principle, that he sent his servant to lay his staff upon a dead child, in order to raise it from the dead; but in this instance the undertaking failed. The Prophet could only resuscitate the child by placing face to face, eye to eye, mouth to mouth, hand to hand, etc., so as to give the greatest possible effect to the imparting of the spirit of life.

For the holy and divine fluid, or spiritual element, to control all other elements, agreeable to its own will, and the will of others, who are in communication or in perfect unison with itself, is just as natural as for the greater to control the less, or the strong the weak. It is upon the same principle that a higher intelligence is able to comprehend, circumscribe, and instruct that which is less.

Hence, when the worlds were framed, God spake, and this divine fluid went forth and executed the mandate, by controlling the elements in accordance with the will, pattern, or designed formed in the mind of him that spake, and it that executed. Wisdom pondered the pattern of all created things, weighed their properties, attributes and uses in the balance of mature intellect. Every minute portion and member of the several departments of life and being, every adaptation to their natural use, was clearly conceived, formed in the mind, and matured, ere the mandate was issued. And the whole was executed in exact accordance with the pattern matured in the divine Mind.

By this divine Spirit all things were designed and formed. By this divine Substance all things live, move, and have a being. By this agency Moses controlled the sea; Joshua the motions of the earth; Daniel the mouths of the lions, and his brethren the flames. By this, the heavens were opened, and were shut; the rain or the dearth prevailed; armies were subdued; the sick healed or the dead raised; and all in accordance with the laws of nature, it being perfectly natural for the subordinate elements to obey the supreme, all-controlling, all-pervading element, which contains in itself the innate and inalienable, controlling power.

The modern world, called "*Christian*," claims to have perpetuated the system called "Christianity," while, at the same time, it declares that the miraculous gifts of the Spirit have ceased.

With as much propriety it might be contended, that the magnet had been perpetuated, but had lost its magnetic properties; that water was perpetuated with all its virtues, but had lost its power to quench thirst, or seek its own level; that fire was still fire, but had lost its heat.

How, we inquire, can Christianity have been perpetuated, while its virtues, its legitimate powers, its distinguishing features, its very life and essence have ceased from among men? Or, of what use is it if it does exist? Is a compass of use when its needle has lost its magnetic attraction? Is water of use when it no longer seeks its level, or quenches thirst? Is fire of use when it loses its heat? Is a sun dial of use on a dark and cloudy day; or a watch without a mainspring?

Or, are the mere forms and ceremonies of any system of use, when the divine, or legitimate powers, for which such forms were instituted, are withdrawn?

O man! be no longer deceived by solemn mockeries of things sacred, or by great and holy names applied to corrupt and degenerate systems.

When the miracles and gifts of the divine Spirit ceased from among men, Christianity ceased, the Christian ministry ceased, the Church of Christ ceased.

That ministry which sets aside modern inspiration, revelation, prophecy, angels, visions, healings, etc., is not ordained of God, but is antichristian in spirit. In short, it is that spirit of priestcraft and kingcraft by which the world, for many ages, has been ruled as with a rod of iron.

The sooner the present generation lose all reverence and respect for modern *"Christianity"* with all its powerless forms and solemn mockeries, the sooner they will be prepared to receive the kingdom of God. The sooner the treasuries of nations, and the purses of individuals, are relieved from the support of priestcraft and superstitions, so much sooner will they be able and willing to devote their means and influence to print and publish the glad tidings of the fullness of the Gospel, restored in this age, to assist in the gathering of the house of Israel, and in the building of the cities and temples of Zion and Jerusalem.

Chapter Twelve

Angels and Spirits

Boast not your lightning wires to hear the news,
Such tardy means the Saints would never choose;
Too slow your fluid, and too short your wires
For heavenly converse, such as love inspires.
If man would fain commune with worlds above,
Angels transport the news on wings of love.

"Are they not all ministering spirits, sent forth to minister for them who shall be heirs of salvation?" (Hebrews 1:14)

Angels are of the same race as men. They are, in fact, men who have passed from the rudimental state to the higher spheres of progressive being. Some have died and risen again to life, and are consequently possessed of a divine, human body of flesh and bones, immortal and eternal. They eat, drink, sing and converse like other men. Some of them hold the keys of Apostleship and Priesthood, by which they teach, instruct, bless, and perform miracles and many mighty works. Translated men, like Enoch, Elijah, John the Apostle, and three of the Apostles of the Western Hemisphere, are also like angels.

Angels are ministers, both to men upon the earth, and to the world of spirits. They pass from one world to another with more ease, and in less time than we pass from one city to another. They have not a single attribute which man has not. But their attributes are more matured, or more developed, than the attributes of men in this present sphere of existence.

Whenever the keys of Priesthood, or, in other words, the keys of the science of Theology, are enjoyed by man on the earth, the people thus privileged, are entitled to the ministering of angels, whose business with men on the earth, is to restore the keys of the Apostleship when lost; to ordain men to the Apostleship when there has been no Apostolic succession: to commit the keys of a new dispensation; to reveal the mysteries of history; the facts of present or past times; and to unfold the events of a future time. They are, sometimes, commissioned also to execute judgments upon individuals, cities or nations. They can be present in their glory, or, they can come in the form and appearance of other men. They can also be present without being visible to mortals.

When they come as other men, they will perhaps eat and drink, and wash their feet; and lodge with their friends. Hence it is written—"*Be not forgetful to entertain strangers: for thereby some have entertained angels unawares.*"

Their business is, also, to comfort and instruct individual members of the Church of the Saints; to heal them by the laying on of hands in the name of Jesus Christ, or to tell them what means to use in order to get well; to teach them good things, to sing them a good song, to warn them of approaching danger, or, to deliver them from prison, or from death.

These blessings have always been enjoyed by the people, or Church of the Saints, whenever such Church has existed on our planet. They are not peculiar to one dispensation more than another.

They were busy in the Patriarchal dispensation, in the Mosaic, and in the Gospel dispensations. They delivered Lot and destroyed Sodom.

They were busy with Moses and the Prophets. They foretold to Zachariah the birth of John. They predicted to Mary her conception, and the birth of Jesus Christ. They informed Joseph, her husband, of her situation. They announced the birth of Jesus to the shepherds of Judea, and sang an anthem of peace on earth and good will to man, to hail him welcome. They attended on his footsteps, in all his sojourn on the earth. In fact, an angel was the instrument to open the gloomy prison of the sepulchre, and to call forth the sleeping body of the Messiah, the first to exclaim, "He is not here, but is risen." Two angels in white raiment, were the first to announce his second advent, while he ascended up in the presence of his disciples. Thus, being delivered from the personal attendance on their Master on the earth, they turned their attention to the Apostles, opened the way for their ministry among Jew and Gentile, delivering them from prison and from danger, and revealing the mysteries which God saw fit to make known to the Saints of that age. And when all the other Apostles had fallen asleep, and the Apostle John had been banished to dig in the coal mines of the lone isle of Patmos, they still were faithful to their charge. They followed him there, and there unfolded to him the events of all ages and generations.

The darkness of the middle ages; the corruptions of Anti-Christ, under the name of Christianity, the rivers of blood, and the oceans of tears, which would flow during eighteen centuries of error; the mighty angel who should again commit the Gospel to the earth, for every nation, kindred, tongue and people; the judgments of God, in the downfall of error and mystery; the restitution or restoration of the Church of the Saints; their final triumph and dominion over the earth; the descent of Jesus Christ to reign over all kingdoms; the resurrection of the Saints, and their reign over the earth, the end of death, and sorrow, and tears, and weeping, were all, all foretold by the angel to the last of the Twelve.

Again, in the present age, have angels restored the Gospel. Again have they committed the keys of Apostleship. Again have they opened some of the events of the past, present, and future.

Again have they attended upon the footsteps of Apostles, Prophets and holy Martyrs, from the cradle to the grave. Again have they aided in the ministry and assisted to deliver from prisons, and from persecutions and death, the Saints of the Most High. And again are they about to execute vengeance on great and notable cities and nations of the earth.

O what an unspeakable blessing is the ministry of angels to mortal man! What a pleasing thought, that many who minister to us, and watch over us, are our near kindred, our fathers who have died and risen again in former ages, and who watch over their descendants with all the parental care and solicitude which characterize affectionate fathers and mothers on the earth.

Thrice happy are they who have lawful claim on their guardianship, and whose conduct does not grieve them, and constrain them to depart from their precious charge.

Spirits are those who have departed this life, and have not yet been raised from the dead.

These are of two kinds, viz.—Good and evil.

These two kinds also include many grades of good and evil.

The good spirits, in the superlative sense of the word, are they who, in this life, partook of the Holy Priesthood, and of the fullness of the Gospel.

This class of spirits minister to the heirs of salvation, both in this world and in the world of spirits. They can appear unto men, when permitted; but not having a fleshly tabernacle, they can not hide their glory. Hence, an unembodied spirit, if it be a holy personage, will be surrounded with a halo of resplendent glory, or brightness, above the brightness of the sun.

Whereas, spirits not worthy to be glorified will appear without this brilliant halo; and although they often attempt to pass as angels of light, there is more or less of darkness about them.

Many spirits of the departed, who are unhappy, linger in lonely wretchedness about the earth, and in the air, and especially about their ancient homesteads, and the places rendered dear to them by the memory of former scenes. The more wicked of these are the kind spoken of in Scripture, as "*foul spirits,*" "*unclean spirits,*" spirits who afflict persons in the flesh, and engender various diseases in the human system. They will sometimes enter human bodies, and will distract them, throw them into fits, cast them into the water, into the fire, etc. They will trouble them with dreams, nightmare, hysterics, fever, etc. They will also deform them in body and in features, by convulsions, cramps, contortions, etc., and will sometimes compel them to utter blasphemies, horrible curses, and even words of other languages. If permitted, they will often cause death. Some of these spirits are adulterous, and suggest to the mind all manner of lasciviousness, all kinds of evil thoughts and temptations.

A person on looking another in the eye, who is possessed of an evil spirit, may feel a shock, a nervous feeling, which will, as it were, make his hair stand on end, in short, a shock resembling that produced in a nervous system by the sight of a serpent.

Some of these foul spirits, when possessing a person, will cause a disagreeable smell about the person thus possessed, which will be plainly manifest to the senses of those about him, even though the person thus afflicted should be washed and change his clothes every few minutes.

There are, in fact, most awful instances of the spirit of lust, and of bawdy and abominable words and actions, inspired and uttered by persons possessed of such spirits, even though the persons were virtuous and modest so long as they possessed their own agency.

Some of these spirits cause deafness, others dumbness, etc.

We can suggest no remedy for these multiplied evils, to which poor human nature is subject, except a good life, while we are in possession of our faculties, prayers and fastings of good and holy men, and the ministry of those who have power given them to rebuke evil spirits, and cast out devils, in the name of Jesus Christ.

Among the diversified spirits abroad in the world there are many religious spirits, which are not of God, but which deceive those who have not the keys of Apostleship and Priesthood, or, in other words, the keys of the science of Theology to guide them. Some of these spirits are manifested in the camp-meetings of certain sects, and in nearly all the excitements and confusions in religious meetings falsely called "*revivals.*" All the strange ecstacies, swoonings, screamings, shoutings, dancings, jumpings, and a thousand other ridiculous and unseemly manifestations, which neither edify nor instruct, are the fruits of these deceptive spirits.

We must, however, pity, rather than ridicule, or despise, the subjects or advocates of these deceptions. Many of them are honest, but they have no Apostles, nor other officers, nor gifts to detect evil, or to keep them from being led by every delusive spirit.

Real visions, or inspirations, which would edify and instruct, they are taught to deny. Should Peter or Paul, or an angel from heaven, come among them, they would denounce him as an impostor, with the assertion that Apostles and angels were no longer needed.

There is still another class of unholy spirits at work in the world— spirits diverse from all these, far more intelligent, and, if possible, still more dangerous. These are, the spirit of divination, vision, foretelling, familiar spirits, "Animal Magnetism," "Mesmerism," etc., which reveal many and great truths mixed with the greatest errors, and also display much intelligence, but have not the keys of the science of Theology—the Holy Priesthood.

These spirits, generally, deny the divinity of Christ, and the great truths of the atonement, and of the resurrection of the body. From this source are all the revelations which deny the ordinances of the Gospel, and the keys and gifts of the Holy Apostleship.

Last of all, these are they who climb up in some other way, besides the door, into the sheepfold; and who prophesy or work in their own name, and not in the name of Jesus Christ.

No man can do a miracle in the name and by the authority of Jesus Christ, except he be a good man, and authorized by Him.

CHAPTER THIRTEEN

Dreams

Mysterious power, whence hope ethereal springs!
Sweet heavenly relic of eternal things!
Inspiring oft deep thoughts of things divine:
The past, the present, and the future thine.
Thy reminiscences transport the soul
To memory's Paradise—its future goal.

*"For God speaketh once, yea twice, yet man perceiveth it not. In a dream,
in a vision of the night, when deep sleep falleth upon men, in slumberings
upon the bed; then he openeth the ears of men, and sealeth their instruction."
(Job 33:14–16)*

In all ages and dispensations God has revealed many important instructions and warnings to men by means of dreams.

When the outward organs of thought and perception are released from their activity, the nerves unstrung, and the whole of mortal humanity lies hushed in quiet slumbers, in order to renew its strength and vigor, it is then that the spiritual organs are at liberty, in a certain degree, to assume their wonted functions, to recall some faint outlines, some confused and half-defined recollections, of that heavenly world, and those endearing scenes of their former estate, from which they have descended in order to obtain and mature a tabernacle of flesh. Their kindred spirits, their guardian angels then hover about them with the fondest affection, the most anxious solicitude. Spirit communes with spirit, thought meets thought, soul blends with soul, in all the raptures of mutual, pure and eternal love.

In this situation the spiritual organs are susceptible of converse with Deity, or of communion with angels and the spirits of just men made perfect.

In this situation we frequently hold communication with our departed father, mother, brother, sister, son or daughter; or with the former husband or wife of our bosom, whose affection for us, being rooted and grounded in the eternal elements, or issuing from under the sanctuary of Love's eternal fountain, can never be lessened or diminished by death, distance of space, or length of years.

We may, perhaps, have had a friend of the other sex, whose pulse beats in unison with our own; whose every thought was big with the aspirations, the hopes of a bright future in union with our own; whose happiness in time or in eternity would never be fully consummated without that union. Such a one, snatched from time in the very bloom of youth, lives in the other sphere, with the same bright hope, watching our every footstep, in our meanderings through the rugged path of life, with longing desires for our eternal happiness, and eager for our safe arrival in the same sphere.

With what tenderness of love, with what solicitude of affection will they watch over our slumbers, hang about our pillow, and seek, by means of the spiritual fluid, to communicate with our spirits, to warn us of dangers or temptation, to comfort and soothe our sorrow, or to ward off the ills which might befall us, or perchance to give us some kind token of remembrance or undying love!

It is the pure in heart, the lovers of truth and virtue, that will appreciate these remarks, for they know, by at least a small degree of experience, that these things are so.

Those who are habitually given to vice, immorality and abomination; those who walk in the daily indulgence of unlawful lust; those who neither believe in Jesus Christ, nor seek to pray to him and keep his commandments; those who do not cultivate the pure, refined and holy joys of innocent and heavenly affection, but who would sacrifice every finer feeling at the shrine of lawless pleasure and brutal desires—those persons will not understand and appreciate these views, because their good angels, their kindred spirits have long since departed, and ceased to attend them, being grieved and disgusted with their conduct.

The Spirit of the Lord has also been grieved, and has left them to themselves, to struggle alone amid the dangers and sorrows of life; or to be the associates of demons and impure spirits. Such persons dream of adultery, gluttony, debauchery and crimes of every kind. Such persons have the foreshadowing of a doleful death, and of darkness, and the buffetings of fiends and malicious spirits.

But, blessed are they who forfeit not their claims to the watchful care and protection of, and communion with, the heavenly powers and pure and lovely spirits.

We can only advise the other classes of mankind, and entreat them, by the joys of love, by all the desires of life, by all the dread of death, darkness, and a dreary hereafter, yea, by the blood of him who died, by the victory of him who rose in triumph from the grave, by their regard for those kindred spirits which would gladly love them in worlds without end, to turn from their sinful course of life, to obey the ordinances and commandments of Jesus Christ, that the Spirit of God may return to them, and their good angels and spirits again return to their sacred charge.

Oh, what a comfort it is, in this dreary world, to be loved and cared for by all-powerful, warm-hearted, and lovely friends!

A Dream!

What have not dreams accomplished?

Dreams and their interpretation brought the beloved son of Jacob from his dungeon, made him prime minister of Egypt, and the savior of a nation, and of his father's house.

Dreams, and the interpretation of dreams, raised a Daniel from slavery or degrading captivity in Babylon, to wear a royal chain of gold, and to teach royalty how to rule, whilst he presided over the governors and presidents of more than a hundred provinces.

Dreams, and the interpretation of dreams, have opened the future, pointed out the course of empire through all the troublous times of successive ages, till Saints alone shall rule, and immortality alone endure.

O, what a doleful situation was Saul the king of Israel placed in, when the army of the Philistines stood in battle array against him, and the Lord answered him not, either by dream, by Prophet, by vision, or by Urim and Thummim!

He sought the unlawful gift of familiar spirits, or "Magnetism." He there learned his doom, and rushed to battle with the desperation of hopeless despair.

Himself, his sons, and the hosts of Israel, fell in battle on that awful day; while David, to whom these gifts had been transferred by the ordination and holy anointing of Samuel, arose by their use to the throne of Israel.

A dream announced by Joseph that his virgin wife should have a son. A dream forewarned him to flee into Egypt with the young child and his mother. A dream announced to him in Egypt the death of Herod, and warned him to return to his native land.

A dream warned the wise men from the east to return home another way, and not return to Herod to betray the young child.

Dreams and visions warned Paul, and the Apostles, and the Saints of his day, of various dangers, shipwrecks, persecutions and deaths, and pointed out the means of escape.

Dreams and visions attended and guided them, more or less, in their whole ministry and sojourn on the earth.

CHAPTER FOURTEEN

The World of Spirits

Ye worlds of light and life, beyond our sphere;
Mysterious country! let your light appear.
Ye angels, lift the veil, the truth unfold,
And give our Seers a glimpse of that bright world;
Tell where ye live, and what is your employ,
Your present blessing, and your future joy.
Say, have you learn'd the name, and tuned the lyre,
And hymn'd the praise of Him—the great Messiah?
Have love's emotions kindled in your breast,
And hope enraptur'd seiz'd the promis'd rest?
Or wait ye still the resurrection day,
That higher promise of Millennial sway?
When Saints and angels come to earth again,
And in the flesh with King Messiah reign?
The spirits answer'd as they soared away—
"We're happy now, but wait a greater day,
When sin and death, and hell, shall conquer'd be,
And *earth*, with heaven, enjoy the victory."

The spirit of man consists of an organization, or embodiment of the elements of spiritual matter, in the likeness and after the pattern of the fleshly tabernacle. It possesses, in fact, all the organs and parts exactly corresponding to the outward tabernacle.

The entrance of this spirit into its embryo tabernacle of flesh, is called quickening. The infallible evidence of its presence is voluntary motion, which implies a degree of independent agency, or inherent will, which individual identity alone possesses.

When this spirit departs, the outward tabernacle is said to be dead, that is, the individual who quickened and imparted voluntary motion to the said tabernacle is no longer there. This individual, on departing from its earthly house, repasses the dark vale of forgetfulness, and awakes in the spirit world.

The spirit world is not the heaven where Jesus Christ, his Father, and other beings dwell, who have, by resurrection or translation, ascended to eternal mansions, and been crowned and seated on thrones of power; but it is an intermediate state, a probation, a place of preparation, improvement, instruction, or education, where spirits are chastened and improved, and where, if found worthy, they may be taught a knowledge of the Gospel. In short, it is a place where the Gospel is preached, and where faith, repentance, hope and charity may be exercised; a place of waiting for the resurrection or redemption of the body; while, to those who deserve it, it is a place of punishment, a purgatory or hell, where spirits are buffeted till the day of redemption.

As to its location, it is here on the very planet where we were born; or, in other words, the earth and other planets of a like sphere, have their inward or spiritual spheres, as well as their outward, or temporal. The one is peopled by temporal tabernacles, and the other by spirits. A veil is drawn between the one sphere and the other, whereby all the objects in the spiritual sphere are rendered invisible to those in the temporal.

To discern beings or things in the spirit world, a person in the flesh must be quickened by spiritual element, the veil must be withdrawn, or the organs of sight, or of hearing, must be transformed, so as to be adapted to the spiritual sphere. This state is called vision, trance, second sight, clairvoyance, etc.

The elements and beings in the spirit world are as real and tangible to spiritual organs, as things and beings of the temporal world are to beings of a temporal state.

In this spirit world there are all the varieties and grades of intellectual being which exist in the present world. For instance, Jesus Christ and the thief on the cross, both went to the same place, and found themselves associated in the spirit world.

But the one was there in all the intelligence, happiness, benevolence, and charity, which characterized a teacher, a messenger, anointed to teach glad tidings to the meek, to bind up the brokenhearted, to comfort those who mourned, to preach deliverance to the captive, and open the prison to those who were bound; or, in other words, *to preach the Gospel to the spirits in prison, that they might be judged according to men in the flesh;* while the other was there as a thief, who had expired on the cross for crime, and who was guilty, ignorant, uncultivated, and unprepared for resurrection, having need of remission of sins, and to be instructed in the science of salvation.

The former bade farewell to the world of spirits on the third day, and returned to his tabernacle of flesh, in which he ascended to thrones, principalities and powers, while the latter is, no doubt, improving in the spirit world, and waiting, believing, hoping for the redemption of the body.

In the world of spirits there are Apostles, Prophets, Elders and members of the Church of the Saints, holding keys of Priesthood, and power to teach, comfort, instruct, and proclaim the Gospel to their fellow-spirits, after the pattern of Jesus Christ.

In the same world there are also the spirits of Catholics, and Protestants of every sect, who have all need to be taught, and to come to the knowledge of the true, unchangeable Gospel, in its fullness and simplicity, that they may be judged the same as if they had been privileged with the same in the flesh.

There is also the Jew, the Mahometan, the infidel, who did not believe in Christ while in the flesh. All these must be taught, must come to the knowledge of the crucified and risen Redeemer, and hear the glad tidings of the Gospel.

There are also all the varieties of the heathen spirits: the noble and refined philosopher, poet, patriot or statesmen of Rome or Greece; the enlightened Socrates, and Plato, and their like, together with every grade of spirits down to the most uncultivated of the savage world.

All these must be taught, enlightened, and must bow the knee to the eternal King, for the decree hath gone forth, that unto him every knee shall bow and every tongue confess.

O what a field of labor, of benevolence, of missionary enterprise now opens to the Apostles and Elders of the Church of the Saints! As this field opens they will begin to realize more fully the extent of their divine mission, and the meaning of the great command to *"Preach the Gospel to every creature."*

In this vast field of labor, the Priesthood are, in a great measure, occupied, during their sojourn in the world of spirits while awaiting the resurrection of the body; and at the same time they themselves are edified, improved, and greatly advanced and matured in the science of divine Theology.

In the use of the keys of this science, by them administered, and in connection with the ministration of certain ordinances, by the Priesthood, in this mortal life, for, and in behalf of, those who are dead, the doors of the prisons of the spirit world are opened, and their gloomy dungeons made radiant with light. Hope then springs afresh. Joy and gladness swell the bosom accustomed to anguish, and smiles assume the place of tears, while songs of triumph, and the voice of melody and thanksgiving occupy the hearts, and flow from the lips, of those who have long dwelt in darkness, and in the region and shadow of death.

The times of sojourn of a spirit in the world of spirits, and also its privileges and degrees of enjoyment or suffering, while there, depend much on its preparations while in the flesh.

For instance, the people swept off by the flood of Noah, were imprisoned in the world of spirits, in a kind of hell; without justification, without Priesthood or Gospel, without the true knowledge of God, or a hope of resurrection, during those long ages which intervened between the flood and the death of Christ. It was only by the personal ministry of the spirit of Jesus Christ, during his sojourn in the spirit world, that they were at length privileged to hear the Gospel, and to act upon their own agency, the same as men in the flesh; whereas, if they had repented at the preaching of Noah, they might have been justified and filled with the hope and knowledge of the resurrection while in the flesh.

When Jesus Christ had returned from his mission in the spirit world, had triumphed over the grave, and re-entered his fleshly tabernacle, then the Saints who had obeyed the Gospel while in the flesh, and had slept in death, or finished their sojourn in the spirit world, were called forth to re-enter their bodies, and to ascend with him to mansions and thrones of eternal power, while the residue of the spirits remained in the world of spirits to await another call.

Those who obeyed the Gospel on the earth, after this first resurrection, will also be called from their sojourn in the spirit world, and reunited with their tabernacles of flesh, at the sounding of the next trump, and will reign on the earth in the flesh one thousand years, while those who rejected the Gospel will remain in the spirit world without a resurrection, till after the thousand years.

Again, those who obey the Gospel in the present age will rise from the spirit world, and from the grave, and reign on the earth during the great thousand years; while those who reject it will remain in condemnation in the spirit world, without a resurrection, till the last trump shall sound, and death and hell deliver up their dead.

CHAPTER FIFTEEN

Resurrection, Its Times and Degrees—First, Second and Third Heavens, or the Telestial, Terrestrial and Celestial Kingdoms

The grave and death and hell no more retain
Their lawful captives. Earth yields its slain.
The raging ocean, from its lowly bed,
At Michael's call, delivers up its dead.
Then come the Judgment, and the final doom
Of man—his destiny beyond the tomb.

There are three general resurrections revealed to man on the earth; one of these is past, and the other two are future.

The first general resurrection took place in connection with the resurrection of Jesus Christ. This included the Saints and Prophets of both hemispheres, from Adam down to John the Baptist; or, in other words, those who died in Christ before his resurrection.

The second will take place in a few years from the present time, and will be immediately succeeded by the coming of Jesus Christ, in power and great glory, with all his Saints and Angels. This resurrection will include the Former and Latter-day Saints—all those who have received the Gospel since the former resurrection.

The last resurrection will take place more than a thousand years afterwards, and will embrace all the human family not included in the former resurrections or translations.

After man is raised from the dead he will be judged according to his works, and will receive the reward, and be consigned to the sphere,

exactly corresponding to his former deeds, and the preparations or qualifications which he possesses.

In the former resurrection, those raised left the earth and ascended,
or, were transplanted far on high, with the risen Jesus, to the glorified
mansions of his Father, or to some planetary system already redeemed
and glorified. The reasons for thus leaving the earth are obvious. Our
planet was still in its rudimental state, and therefore subject to the rule of
sin and death. It was necessary that it should continue thus, until the full
time of redemption should arrive; it was, therefore, entirely unfitted for
the residence of immortal man.

But in the resurrection which now approaches, and in connection
with the glorious coming of Jesus Christ, the earth will undergo a change
in its physical features, climate, soil, productions; and in its political,
moral and spiritual government.

Its mountains will be leveled, its valleys exalted, its swamps and sickly
places will be drained and become healthy, while its burning deserts, and its
frigid polar regions, will be redeemed and become temperate and fruitful.

Kingcraft and priestcraft, tyranny, oppression and idolatry will be at
an end, darkness and ignorance will pass away, war will cease, and the
rule of sin, and sorrow, and death will give place to the reign of peace, and
truth, and righteousness.

For this reason, and to fulfill certain promises made to the Fathers,
the Former and Latter-day Saints included in the two resurrections, and
all those translated, will then receive an inheritance on the earth, and will
build upon and improve the same for a thousand years.

The heathen nations, also, will then be redeemed, and will be exalted
to the privilege of serving the Saints of the Most High. They will be the
ploughmen, the vine-dressers, the gardeners, builders, etc. But the Saints
will be the owners of the soil, the proprietors of all real estate, and other
precious things, and the kings, governors and judges of the earth.

As the children of man multiply in those peaceful times, a careful
and wise system of agriculture will be rapidly developed, and extended
over the face of the whole earth; its entire surface will at length become
like the Garden of Eden, the trees of life being cultivated, and their fruits
enjoyed.

Science, and the useful and ornamental arts, will also be greatly
extended and cultivated. The fine-toned instrument of many strings, the
melodious organs of the human voice, will then be tuned to poetry and

sentiments equally pure and refined, and will pour forth melodies and strains of holy joy, calculated to purify and melt every heart in love, and fill every soul with mutual sympathy and ecstasy of heavenly union.

Geographical knowledge, history, astronomy, mathematics and navigation will be greatly extended and matured. Railroads and telegraphic lines of communication will be universally extended, and the powers of steam, or other means of locomotion brought to the highest state of perfection.

Thus all nations will be associated in one great brotherhood. A universal Theocracy will cement the whole body politic. One King will rule. One holy city will compose the capital. One temple will be the centre of worship. In short, there will be one Lord, one Faith, one Baptism and one Spirit.

One equable, just and useful commercial interest, founded on the necessity and convenience of mutual exchange of products, will also form another important bond of union.

Mineralogy will also be greatly improved, and its knowledge extended. Its hidden treasures will be developed, and gold, silver and the most precious and beautiful stones will be the building materials in most common use, and will compose the utensils and furniture of the habitations of man.

The earth and man, thus restored and exalted, will not yet be perfect in the celestial sense of the word, but will be considered, in the light of eternity, as occupying an intermediate and still progressive position amid the varieties of nature.

The flesh, bones, sinews, nerves—all the organs—all the particles of the celestial body, must be quickened, filled, surrounded with that divine and holy element, which is purer, more intelligent, more refined and active, fuller of light and life than any other substance in the universe.

Every organ must be restored, and adapted to its natural and perfect use in the celestial body.

> The Greek philosopher's immortal hand,
> Again with flesh and bone and nerve combined;
> Immortal brain and heart—immortal whole,
> Will make, as at the first, a living soul.

Man, thus adapted to all the enjoyments of life and love, will possess the means of gratifying his organs of sight, hearing, taste, etc., and will possess, improve and enjoy the riches of the eternal elements. The palace, the city, the garden, the vineyard, the fruits of the earth, the gold, the silver, the precious stones, the servants, the chariots, horses and horsemen are for his use; also thrones and dominions, principalities and powers, might, majesty, and an eternal increase of riches, honors, immortality, and eternal life are his. He is, in a subordinate sense, a god: or in other words, one of the sons of God. All things are his, and he is Christ's, and Christ is God's.

Such is the great Millennium.

And such is *celestial* man, in his progress toward perfection.

Besides the peculiar glory of the *celestial,* there are in the resurrection and final reward of man, many subordinate spheres, many degrees of reward adapted to an almost infinite variety of circumstances, conditions, degrees of improvement, knowledge, accountability and conduct.

The final state of man, though varying in almost infinite gradations and rewards, adapted to his qualifications and deserts, and meted out in the scale of exact justice and mercy, may be conceived or expressed under three grand heads or principal spheres, viz.—

First. The Telestial, or least heaven, typified by the stars of the firmament.

Secondly. The Terrestrial, or intermediate heaven, typified by the moon.

Thirdly. The Celestial, or third heaven, of which the sun of the firmament is typical.

The qualifications which fit and prepare intelligences, for these different spheres or rewards, are an all-important consideration, and well worthy of the sincere attention of all people.

These several kingdoms or degrees, and their comparative happiness, and what characters are candidates for each degree, are revealed in a most concise, clear, lucid and beautiful manner, in one of the visions of our great Prophet and founder. We will therefore complete this chapter by the insertion of said

VISION

"Hear, O ye heavens, and give ear, O earth, and rejoice ye inhabitants thereof, for the Lord is God, and beside him there is no Savior.

"Great is his wisdom, marvelous are his ways, and the extent of his doings none can find out.

"His purposes fail not, neither are there any who can stay his hand.

"From eternity to eternity he is the same, and his years never fail.

"For thus saith the Lord—I, the Lord, am merciful and gracious unto those who fear me, and delight to honor those who serve me in righteousness and in truth unto the end.

"Great shall be their reward and eternal shall be their glory.

"And to them will I reveal all mysteries, yea, all the hidden mysteries of my kingdom from days of old, and for ages to come, will I make known unto them the good pleasure of my will concerning all things pertaining to my kingdom.

"Yea, even the wonders of eternity shall they know, and things to come will I show them, even the things of many generations.

"And their wisdom shall be great, and their understanding reach to heaven; and before them the wisdom of the wise shall perish, and the understanding of the prudent shall come to naught.

"For by my Spirit will I enlighten them, and by my power will I make known unto them the secrets of my will—yea, even those things which eye has not seen, nor ear heard, nor yet entered into the heart of man.

"We, Joseph Smith, Jun., and Sidney Rigdon, being in the Spirit on the sixteenth day of February, in the year of our Lord one thousand eight hundred and thirty-two—

"By the power of the Spirit our eyes were opened and our understandings were enlightened, so as to see and understand the things of God—

"Even those things which were from the beginning before the world was, which were ordained of the Father, through his Only Begotten Son, who was in the bosom of the Father, even from the beginning;

"Of whom we bear record; and the record which we bear is the fulness of the gospel of Jesus Christ, who is the Son, whom we saw and with whom we conversed in the heavenly vision.

"For while we were doing the work of translation, which the Lord had appointed unto us, we came to the twenty-ninth verse of the fifth chapter of John, which was given unto us as follows—

"Speaking of the resurrection of the dead, concerning those who shall hear the voice of the Son of Man:

"And shall come forth; they who have done good in the resurrection of the just; and they who have done evil, in the resurrection of the unjust.

"Now this caused us to marvel, for it was given unto us of the Spirit.

"And while we meditated upon these things, the Lord touched the eyes of our understandings and they were opened, and the glory of the Lord shone round about.

"And we beheld the glory of the Son, on the right hand of the Father, and received of his fulness;

"And saw the holy angels, and them who are sanctified before his throne, worshiping God, and the Lamb, who worship him forever and ever.

"And now, after the many testimonies which have been given of him, this is the testimony, last of all, which we give of him: That he lives!

"For we saw him, even on the right hand of God; and we heard the voice bearing record that he is the Only Begotten of the Father—

"That by him, and through him, and of him, the worlds are and were created, and the inhabitants thereof are begotten sons and daughters unto God.

"And this we saw also, and bear record, that an angel of God who was in authority in the presence of God, who rebelled against the Only Begotten Son whom the Father loved and who was in the bosom of the Father, was thrust down from the presence of God and the Son,

"And was called Perdition, for the heavens wept over him—he was Lucifer, a son of the morning.

"And we beheld, and lo, he is fallen! is fallen, even a son of the morning!

"And while we were yet in the Spirit, the Lord commanded us that we should write the vision; for we beheld Satan, that old serpent, even the devil, who rebelled against God, and sought to take the kingdom of our God and his Christ—

"Wherefore, he maketh war with the saints of God, and encompasseth them round about.

"And we saw a vision of the sufferings of those with whom he made war and overcame, for thus came the voice of the Lord unto us:

"Thus saith the Lord concerning all those who know my power, and have been made partakers thereof, and suffered themselves through the power of the devil to be overcome, and to deny the truth and defy my power—

"They are they who are the sons of perdition, of whom I say that it had been better for them never to have been born;

"For they are vessels of wrath, doomed to suffer the wrath of God, with the devil and his angels in eternity;

"Concerning whom I have said there is no forgiveness in this world nor in the world to come—

"Having denied the Holy Spirit after having received it, and having denied the Only Begotten Son of the Father, having crucified him unto themselves and put him to an open shame.

"These are they who shall go away into the lake of fire and brimstone, with the devil and his angels—

"And the only ones on whom the second death shall have any power;

"Yea, verily, the only ones who shall not be redeemed in the due time of the Lord, after the sufferings of his wrath.

"For all the rest shall be brought forth by the resurrection of the dead, through the triumph and the glory of the Lamb, who was slain, who was in the bosom of the Father before the worlds were made.

"And this is the gospel, the glad tidings, which the voice out of the heavens bore record unto us—

"That he came into the world, even Jesus, to be crucified for the world, and to bear the sins of the world, and to sanctify the world, and to cleanse it from all unrighteousness;

"That through him all might be saved whom the Father had put into his power and made by him;

"Who glorifies the Father, and saves all the works of his hands, except those sons of perdition who deny the Son after the Father has revealed him.

"Wherefore, he saves all except them—they shall go away into ever-lasting punishment, which is endless punishment, which is eternal punishment, to reign with the devil and his angels in eternity, where their worm dieth not, and the fire is not quenched, which is their torment—

"And the end thereof, neither the place thereof, nor their torment, no man knows;

"Neither was it revealed, neither is, neither will be revealed unto man, except to them who are made partakers thereof;

"Nevertheless, I, the Lord, show it by vision unto many, but straight-way shut it up again;

"Wherefore, the end, the width, the height, the depth, and the misery thereof, they understand not, neither any man except those who are ordained unto this condemnation.

"And we heard the voice, saying: Write the vision, for lo, this is the end of the vision of the sufferings of the ungodly.

"And again we bear record—for we saw and heard, and this is the testimony of the gospel of Christ concerning them who shall come forth in the resurrection of the just—

"They are they who received the testimony of Jesus, and believed on his name and were baptized after the manner of his burial, being buried in the water in his name, and this according to the commandment which he has given—

"That by keeping the commandments they might be washed and cleansed from all their sins, and receive the Holy Spirit by the laying on of the hands of him who is ordained and sealed unto this power;

"And who overcome by faith, and are sealed by the Holy Spirit of promise, which the Father sheds forth upon all those who are just and true.

"They are they who are the church of the Firstborn.

"They are they into whose hands the Father has given all things—

"They are they who are priests and kings, who have received of his fulness, and of his glory;

"And are priests of the Most High, after the order of Melchizedek, which was after the order of Enoch, which was after the order of the Only Begotten Son.

"Wherefore, as it is written, they are gods, even the sons of God—

"Wherefore, all things are theirs, whether life or death, or things present, or things to come, all are theirs and they are Christ's, and Christ is God's.

"And they shall overcome all things.

"Wherefore, let no man glory in man, but rather let him glory in God, who shall subdue all enemies under his feet.

"These shall dwell in the presence of God and his Christ forever and ever.

"These are they whom he shall bring with him, when he shall come in the clouds of heaven to reign on the earth over his people.

"These are they who shall have part in the first resurrection.

"These are they who shall come forth in the resurrection of the just.

"These are they who are come unto Mount Zion, and unto the city of the living God, the heavenly place, the holiest of all.

"These are they who have come to an innumerable company of angels, to the general assembly and church of Enoch, and of the Firstborn.

"These are they whose names are written in heaven, where God and Christ are the judge of all.

"These are they who are just men made perfect through Jesus the mediator of the new covenant, who wrought out this perfect atonement through the shedding of his own blood.

"These are they whose bodies are celestial, whose glory is that of the sun, even the glory of God, the highest of all, whose glory the sun of the firmament is written of as being typical.

"And again, we saw the terrestrial world, and behold and lo, these are they who are of the terrestrial, whose glory differs from that of the church of the Firstborn who have received the fulness of the Father, even as that of the moon differs from the sun in the firmament.

"Behold, these are they who died without law;

"And also they who are the spirits of men kept in prison, whom the Son visited, and preached the gospel unto them, that they might be judged according to men in the flesh;

"Who received not the testimony of Jesus in the flesh, but afterwards received it.

"These are they who are honorable men of the earth, who were blinded by the craftiness of men.

"These are they who receive of his glory, but not of his fulness.

"These are they who receive of the presence of the Son, but not of the fulness of the Father.

"Wherefore, they are bodies terrestrial, and not bodies celestial, and differ in glory as the moon differs from the sun.

"These are they who are not valiant in the testimony of Jesus; wherefore, they obtain not the crown over the kingdom of our God.

"And now this is the end of the vision which we saw of the terrestrial, that the Lord commanded us to write while we were yet in the Spirit.

"And again, we saw the glory of the telestial, which glory is that of the lesser, even as the glory of the stars differs from that of the glory of the moon in the firmament.

"These are they who received not the gospel of Christ, neither the testimony of Jesus.

"These are they who deny not the Holy Spirit.

"These are they who are thrust down to hell.

"These are they who shall not be redeemed from the devil until the last resurrection, until the Lord, even Christ the Lamb, shall have finished his work.

"These are they who receive not of his fulness in the eternal world, but of the Holy Spirit through the ministration of the terrestrial;

"And the terrestrial through the ministration of the celestial.

"And also the telestial receive it of the administering of angels who are appointed to minister for them, or who are appointed to be ministering spirits for them; for they shall be heirs of salvation.

"And thus we saw, in the heavenly vision, the glory of the telestial, which surpasses all understanding;

"And no man knows it except him to whom God has revealed it.

"And thus we saw the glory of the terrestrial which excels in all things the glory of the telestial, even in glory, and in power, and in might, and in dominion.

"And thus we saw the glory of the celestial, which excels in all things— where God, even the Father, reigns upon his throne forever and ever;

"Before whose throne all things bow in humble reverence, and give him glory forever and ever.

"They who dwell in his presence are the church of the Firstborn; and they see as they are seen, and know as they are known, having received of his fulness and of his grace;

"And he makes them equal in power, and in might, and in dominion.

"And the glory of the celestial is one, even as the glory of the sun is one.

"And the glory of the terrestrial is one, even as the glory of the moon is one.

"And the glory of the telestial is one, even as the glory of the stars is one; for as one star differs from another star in glory, even so differs one from another in glory in the telestial world;

"For these are they who are of Paul, and of Apollos, and of Cephas.

"These are they who say they are some of one and some of another— some of Christ and some of John, and some of Moses, and some of Elias, and some of Esaias, and some of Isaiah, and some of Enoch;

"But received not the gospel, neither the testimony of Jesus, neither the prophets, neither the everlasting covenant.

"Last of all, these all are they who will not be gathered with the saints, to be caught up unto the church of the Firstborn, and received into the cloud.

"These are they who are liars, and sorcerers, and adulterers, and whoremongers, and whosoever loves and makes a lie.

"These are they who suffer the wrath of God on earth.

"These are they who suffer the vengeance of eternal fire.

"These are they who are cast down to hell and suffer the wrath of Almighty God, until the fulness of times, when Christ shall have subdued all enemies under his feet, and shall have perfected his work;

"When he shall deliver up the kingdom, and present it unto the Father, spotless, saying: I have overcome and have trodden the wine-press alone, even the wine-press of the fierceness of the wrath of Almighty God.

"Then shall he be crowned with the crown of his glory, to sit on the throne of his power to reign forever and ever.

"But behold, and lo, we saw the glory and the inhabitants of the telestial world, that they were as innumerable as the stars in the firmament of heaven, or as the sand upon the seashore;

"And heard the voice of the Lord saying: These all shall bow the knee, and every tongue shall confess to him who sits upon the throne forever and ever;

"For they shall be judged according to their works, and every man shall receive according to his own works, his own dominion, in the mansions which are prepared;

"And they shall be servants of the Most High; but where God and Christ dwell they cannot come, worlds without end.

"This is the end of the vision which we saw, which we were commanded to write while we were yet in the Spirit.

"But great and marvelous are the works of the Lord, and the mysteries of his kingdom which he showed unto us, which surpass all understanding in glory, and in might, and in dominion;

"Which he commanded us we should not write while we were yet in the Spirit, and are not lawful for man to utter;

"Neither is man capable to make them known, for they are only to be seen and understood by the power of the Holy Spirit, which God bestows on those who love him, and purify themselves before him;

"To whom he grants this privilege of seeing and knowing for themselves;

"That through the power and manifestation of the Spirit, while in the flesh, they may be able to bear his presence in the world of glory.

"And to God and the Lamb be glory, and honor, and dominion forever and ever. Amen." (D&C 76.)

CHAPTER SIXTEEN

Further Remarks on Man's Physical and Intellectual Progress—Philosophy of Will, as Originating, Directing, and Controlling All Voluntary Animal Motion—Astounding Facts in Relation to the Speed or Velocity of Motion, as Attainable by Physical Man—Intercommunication of the Inhabitants of Different and Distant Planets

Wide, and more wide, the kindling bosom swells,
As love inspires, and truth its wonders tell,
The soul enraptured tunes the sacred lyre,
And bids a worm of earth to heaven aspire,
'Mid solar systems numberless, to soar,
The depths of love and science to explore.

As I have before remarked, man is a candidate for a series of progressive changes, all tending to develop his intellectual and physical faculties, to expand his mind, and to enlarge his sphere of action and consequent usefulness and happiness.

He begins his physical, or rudimental, fleshly career by descending below all things. He has at his birth less power of locomotion, or even instinct, than other animals.

His powers of motion are so very limited, that for several months he is entirely unable to change his locality. Wherever he is placed, there he must remain until removed by the agency of others. He can hardly be said to have a will, or, at least, it is so undeveloped as scarcely to manifest itself by any effort beyond the movement of some portion of his members. While he remains in this state of mental inability and physical helplessness, a casual observer, entirely unacquainted with his progress and destiny, might very naturally conclude that this was the climax of his maturity, the natural sphere of his eternal existence.

A few months, however, develop a marked change—he begins to learn the use, and put forth the powers of his will. The body, developed in a commensurate degree, is able to obey that will. Thus commences locomotion. The child crawls or creeps about the floor, explores the little world—that is to say, the room where he resides, or the adjoining apartment—becomes familiar with its dimensions, bearings and contents, and recognizes his associates or fellow citizens of the same little world. Then he becomes familiar with the science of geography and of history, if I may so call it, in his little world.

Prompted by curiosity, he may, perhaps, cast an occasional glance beyond the limits of his own abode. He may contemplate a building or landscape on the other side of the street or field, but with much of the same feeling as a man, more matured, casts his eyes to the distant planets. He concludes that these distant objects are entirely beyond the reach of his powers of locomotion.

In a short time, however, his faculties, still expanding, develop new and increasing energies. He conceives *"big thoughts."* He even thinks of dispensing with his plodding, creeping manner of locomotion, and of trying to stand upright, and even makes a first step towards walking. It is a great undertaking. He hesitates, doubts, fears, hopes till finally, being cheered onward in his career by his parents or his nurse, he makes the attempt. After several falls, failures, and disappointments, he at length succeeds in walking two or three steps. O what a triumph in his powers of locomotion! He is cheered, embraced, overwhelmed, by those who have been watching his progress and encouraging him, until, overcome and carried away by an ecstasy of transport, he falls, blushing, smiling and exulting into the arms held out for his reception. He dreams not of a higher attainment. He is now, in his own estimation, at the very highest pinnacle of human development.

Improving in his new mode of locomotion, he soon runs about the yard, along the street, through the field, makes new discoveries, sees new habitations, enlarges his geographical knowledge, and begins to conceive the probability that his views have been too narrow, and that there may be a bigger world, more people, and more buildings than were dreamed of in his philosophy.

In a few years he may become familiar with the geography and history of the island or continent on which he lives. He may even begin to aspire after the knowledge of other climes, and to conceive or conjecture that beyond the limits of the almost infinite expanse of waters, things and beings may exist after the similitude of his own sphere, He longs to overcome the physical barriers which confine him in so limited a sphere, and thus enlarge his acquaintance, his social feelings, his friendship, his affections and his scientific knowledge.

So boundless and varied is the field, so complicated are the obstacles to be surmounted, so vast the preparations, improvements and inventions to be brought into requisition, that after ages and generations have exhausted their energies, much is still left to be done—much which can only be done by the progress and extension of those modern triumphs of art by which the elements—the fire, the wind, the water, the lightning, submit to the control of man, and become his chariot, his bearer of dispatches. By these means the globe we occupy will soon be explored, the limits, boundaries and resources of every dark corner be clearly defined and understood.

Man already moves over the surface of the earth at the rate of fifty, sixty and even ninety miles per hour, and still he aspires. He contemplates making the air his chariot, and wafting himself through the open firmament at the rate of perhaps a thousand miles per hour. Suppose he attains to this, what then? Will the great, the infinite principle within him be satisfied? No. He lifts his eyes to the contemplation of those myriads of shining orbs on high. He knows by actual admeasurement that some of them are much larger than the planet he occupies. He also knows by analogy that eternal riches are there; that a boundless store of element and resources is there; that they are treasured there for the use, comfort, convenience and enjoyment of intellectual and physical beings—beings, for aught he knows, of his own species, and connected with him by kindred ties, or by the law of universal sympathy and affection. He has reason to believe that there are gold and silver, that there are precious stones, and houses, and cities, and gardens. That there are walks of pleasure, and fountains, forests, brooks and rivers of delight; that there are bosoms fraught with life and joy, and swelling with all the tender sensibilities of a pure, holy and never-ending affection.

Why, then, should his aspirations not reach forth, his mind expand, his bosom swell with love, and his heart beat with the boundless, fathomless,

infinitude of thought, of feeling and of love? Why not be noble and boundless in charity, like the God whom he calls his Father? Why does he not rise
from his groveling sphere in the small island, which floats in the ocean of
space as a small black speck, amid the numberless shining orbs? The reason
is obvious; it is not for the want of noble aspirations; it is not for the want
of grand conceptions; it is not for the lack of will. It is because the body is
chained, imprisoned, confined here by the operation or attraction of surrounding elements which man has not yet discovered the means to control.
It may be said that the powers of earth enslave him and chain him down,
beyond the possibility or hope of escape.

Reader, in order to illustrate this subject, try an experiment on your
own physical and mental powers. For instance, *will* your arm to move,
and it will instantly obey you. *Will* your body to go three miles, and it will
obey you as fast as it can; perhaps in one hour it will have accomplished
the journey assigned to it by your will.

But tie your hand behind you and then *will* it to move up and down,
forward and backward, and it will make the effort to obey you, but cannot
because it is confined. Chain your body in a dungeon, bolt and bar the
door, and *will* it to a certain place, and it will not obey you, because it is
physically incapable.

Unchain this body, provide the means of conveyance at the rate of
a mile per minute; the body, at the bidding of the *will*, will then go the
three miles in three minutes.

Now, if it were possible to overcome the resisting elements, so as to
increase the speed of conveyance of your body, that is, if there were no
resisting element to be overcome, your will might dictate and your body
would move through actual space with the speed of light or electricity. There is no apparent limit to the speed attainable by the body when
unchained, set free from the elements which now enslave it, and dictated
by the will.

"The lighting on its wiry way would lag behind,
The sun-ray drag its slow length along."

This immense velocity of locomotion, as applied to a body of flesh
and bones, or of material elements, may, at first thought, strike the mind
as being contrary to the known laws of physical motion.

But let it be recollected that the vast earth on which we dwell, with all its weight and bulk, its cities, animals and intelligences, moves through actual space at the astonishing velocity of eighteen miles per second, one thousand and eighty miles per minute, or sixty-four thousand eight hundred miles per hour.

If so vast a bulk of gross, and in a great measure inanimate matter, can move through space at a rate of speed so inconceivably great, how easily we can conceive the probability of vastly increased powers of loco-motion on the part of animate bodies released from their earthly prison, quickened by superior and celestial element, dictated by an independent, inherent principle called the will, and urged onward by the promptings of the eternal, infinite mind and affections, in their aspirations for knowledge and enjoyment.

A corporeal, human body, raised from the dead, and quickened by elements so refined, so full of life and motion, so pure, and so free from the influences, control, or attractions of more gross elements, will, like the risen Jesus, ascend and descend at will, and with a speed nearly instantaneous.

Let us pause, and contemplate, for a moment, such a being taking leave of the confines of the earth, and sea, and clouds, and air, with all their dark and gloomy shadows. Behold him as he speeds his way on the upper deep, and launches forth in the clear and boundless expanse bespangled with millions of resplendent orbs.

He calculates his distance, and regulates his course by observing the relative position of those most familiar to him, and, soaring upwards still, his bosom swells with an unutterable and overwhelming sensation of the infinitude of his own eternal being, and of all around, above, below him, till, unable to contain his gratitude, and joy, and exultation, he breaks forth in the language of a celebrated British poet, and sings as he flies—

"Heaven's broad day hath o'er me broken,
Far above earth's span of sky!
Am I dead? Nay, by this token,
Know that I have ceased to die!"

Planets will be visited, messages communicated, acquaintances and friendships formed, and the sciences vastly extended and cultivated.

The science of geography will then be extended to millions of worlds, and will embrace a knowledge of their physical features and boundaries, their resources, mineral and vegetable; their rivers, lakes, seas, continents and islands; the attainments of their inhabitants in the science of government; their progress in revealed religion; their employments, dress, manners, customs, etc. The science of astronomy will also be enlarged in proportion to the means of knowledge. System after system will rise to view in the vast field of research and exploration! Vast systems of suns and their attendant worlds, on which the eyes of Adam's race, in their rudimental sphere, have never gazed, will then be contemplated, circumscribed, weighed in the balance of human thought, their circumference and diameter be ascertained, their relative distances understood. Their motions and revolutions, their times and laws, their hours, days, weeks, sabbaths, months, years, jubilees, centuries, millenniums and eternities, will all be told in the volumes of science.

The science of history will embrace the vast "univercoelum" of the past and present. It will, in its vast compilations, embrace and include all nations, all ages, and all generations; all the planetary systems in all their varied progress and changes, in all their productions and attributes.

It will trace our race in all its successive emigrations, colonies, states, kingdoms and empires; from their first existence on the great, central, governing planet, or sun, called Kolob, until they are increased without number, and widely dispersed and transplanted from one planet to another, until, occupying the very confines of infinitude, the mind of immortal, eternal man, is absorbed, overwhelmed, wearied with the vastness, the boundless expanse of historic fact, and compelled to return and retire within itself for refreshment, rest and renewed vigor.

Next in order, will be the field of prophetic science. The spirit of prophecy will be poured upon the immortal mind, till, from seeing in part, and knowing in part, man will be able to gaze upon a boundless prospective, a future of still increasing glory, knowledge, light, love, might, majesty, power and dominion, in which the sons of God, the kings, and priests of heaven and earth, and of the heaven of heavens, and all their retinue of kingdoms and subjects, will find ample room for boundless increase and improvement, worlds without end. Amen.

CHAPTER SEVENTEEN

Laws of Marriage and Procreation

Ye kindred spirits, filled with mutual love,
Pure as the dews descending from above,
All hail! for you the sacred keys are given,
To make you one on earth, and one in heaven.
Be fruitful then, and let your race extend;
Fill earth, the stars, and worlds that never end.

The great science of life consists in the knowledge of ourselves, the laws of our existence, the relations we sustain to each other, to things and beings around us, to our ancestry, to our posterity, to time, to eternity, to our heavenly Father and to the universe.

To understand these laws, and regulate our actions by them, is the whole duty of intelligences. It should therefore comprise our whole study.

This science comprises the fountain of wisdom, the well-springs of life, the boundless ocean of knowledge, the infinitude of light, the truth, and love. It penetrates the depths, soars to the heights, and circumscribes the broad expanse of eternity.

Its pursuit leads to exaltation, glory, immortality, and to an eternity of life, light, purity, and unity of fellowship with kindred spirits.

To contemplate man in his true light, we must, as it were, forget that death is in his path; we must look upon him as an eternal, ever-living being, possessing spirit, flesh and bones, with all the mental and physical organs, and all the affections and sympathies which characterize him in this world. Or rather, all his natural affections and sympathies will be purified, exalted, and immeasurably increased.

Let the candidate for celestial glory forget, for a moment, the groveling sphere of his present existence, and make the effort to contemplate himself in the light of eternity, in the higher spheres of his progressive existence, beyond the grave—a pure spirit, free from sin and guile, enlightened in the school of heaven, by observation and experience, and association with the highest order of intelligences, for thousands of years; and clothed with immortal flesh, in all the vigor, freshness and beauty of eternal youth; free alike from pain, disease, death, and the corroding effects of time; looking back through the vista of far distant years, and contemplating his former sojourn amid the sorrows and pains of mortal life, his passage through the dark valley of death, and his sojourn in the spirit world, as we now contemplate a transient dream, or a night of sleep, from which we have awakened, renewed and refreshed, to enter again upon the realities of life.

Let us contemplate, for a moment, such a being, clothed in the finest robes of linen, pure and white, adorned with precious stones and gold; a countenance radiant with the effulgence of light, intelligence and love; a bosom glowing with all the confidence of conscious innocence, dwelling in palaces of precious stones and gold; bathing in the crystal waters of life; promenading or sitting 'neath the evergreen bowers and trees of Eden; inhaling the healthful breezes, perfumed with odor, wafted from the roses and pinks of paradise, or assembled with the countless myriads of heaven's nobility, to join in songs of praise and adoration to the Great Parent of every good, to tune the immortal lyre in strains celestial; or move with grace immortal to the soul-inspiring measure of music flowing from a thousand instruments, blending, in harmonious numbers, with celestial voices, in heavenly song, or mingling in graceful circles with joyous thousands, immersed in the same spirit, and moving in unison and harmony of motion, as if one heart, one pulse, one thrill of heavenly melody inspired the whole.

O candidates for celestial glory! Would your joys be full in the countless years of eternity without forming the connections, the relationship, the kindred ties which concentrate in the domestic circle, and branch forth, and bud and blossom, and bear the fruits of eternal increase?

Would that eternal emotion of charity and benevolence which swells your bosoms be satisfied to enjoy in "single blessedness," without an increase of posterity, those exhaustless stores of never ending riches and enjoyments? Or, would you, like your heavenly Father, prompted by eternal benevolence and charity, wish to fill countless millions of worlds, with your begotten sons and daughters, and to bring them through all the gradations of progressive being, to inherit immortal bodies and eternal mansions in your Several dominions?

If such be your aspirations, remember that this present probation is the world of preparation for joys eternal. This is the place where family organization is first formed for eternity; and where the kindred sympathies, relationships and affections take root spring forth, shoot upward, bud, blossom and bear fruit to ripen and mature in eternal ages.

Here, in the holy temples and sanctuaries of our God, must the everlasting covenants be revealed, ratified, sealed, bound and recorded in the holy records, and guarded and preserved in the archives of God's Kingdom, by those who hold the keys of eternal Apostleship, who have power to bind on earth that which shall be bound in heaven, and to record on earth that which shall be recorded in the archives of heaven, in the Lamb's book of life.

Here, in the holy sanctuary, must be revealed, ordained and anointed the kings and queens of eternity.

All vows, covenants, contracts, marriages, of unions, not formed by revelation, and sealed for time and all eternity, and recorded in the holy archives of earth and heaven, by the ministration of the holy and eternal PRIESTHOOD, will be dissolved by death, and will not be recognized by the eternal authorities, after the parties have entered through the veil into the eternal world.

This is heaven's eternal law, as revealed to the ancients of all ages, who held the keys of eternal Priesthood, after the order of the Son of God; and, as restored with the Priesthood of the Saints of this age.

Strict laws were also given and diligently taught to both sexes, regulating the intercourse between husband and wife. All intercourse peculiar to the sexes was strictly prohibited at certain seasons which were untimely. Nor were the bonds of wedlock any shield from condemnation, where the parties, by untimely union, excess or voluntary act, prevented propagation, or injured the life or health of themselves or their offspring.

The object of the Union of the sexes is the propagation of their species, or procreation; also for mutual affection, and the cultivation of those eternal principles of never ending charity and benevolence, which are inspired by the Eternal Spirit; also for mutual comfort and assistance in this world of toil and sorrow, and for mutual duties toward their offspring.

Marriage, and its duties, are therefore, not a mere matter of choice or convenience, or of pleasure to the parties; but to marry and multiply is a positive command of Almighty God, binding on all persons of both sexes who are circumstanced and conditioned to fulfill the same. To marry, propagate our species, do our duty to them, and to educate them in the light of truth, are among the chief objects of our existence on the earth. To neglect these duties, is to fail to answer the end of our creation, and is a very great sin.

While to pervert our natures, and to prostitute ourselves and our strength to mere pleasures, or to unlawful communion of the sexes, is alike subversive of health, of pure, holy and lasting affection; of moral and social order; and of the laws of God and nature.

If we except murder, there is scarcely a more damning sin on the earth than the prostitution of female virtue or chastity at the shrine of pleasure, or brutal lust; or that promiscuous and lawless intercourse which chills and corrodes the heart, perverts and destroys the pure affections, cankers and destroys, as it were, the well-springs, the fountains, or issues of life.

A man who obeys the ordinances of God, and is without blemish or deformity, who has sound health and mature age, and enjoys liberty and access to the elements of life, is designed to be the head of a woman, a father, and a guide of the weaker sex, and of those of tender age, to mansions of eternal life and salvation.

A woman, under similar circumstances, is designed to be the glory of some man in the Lord; to be led and governed by him as her head in all things, even as Christ is the head of the man; to honor, obey, love, serve, comfort and help him in all things; to be a happy wife, and, if blessed with offspring, a faithful and affectionate mother, devoting her life to the joys, cares and duties of her domestic sphere.

The false and corrupt institutions, and still more corrupt practices of "*Christendom*," have had a downward tendency in the generations of man for many centuries. Our physical organization, health, vigor, strength of body, intellectual faculties, inclinations etc., are influenced very much by parentage. Hereditary disease, idiocy, weakness of mind, or of constitution, deformity, tendency to violent and ungovernable passions, vicious appetites and desires, are often engendered by parents; and are bequeathed as a heritage from generation to generation. Man becomes a murderer, a thief, an adulterer, a drunkard, a lover of tobacco, opium, or other nauseous or poisonous drugs, by means of the predisposition, and inclinations engendered by parentage.

The people before the flood, and also the Sodomites and Canaanites, had carried these corruptions and degeneracies so far that God, in mercy, destroyed them, and thus put an end to the procreation of races so degenerate and abominable; while Noah, Abraham, Melchizedek and others, who were taught in the true laws of procreation, *were perfect in their generation,* and trained their children in the same laws.

The overthrow of those ancient degenerate races is a type of that which now awaits the nations called *"Christian,"* or, in other words, *"the great whore of all the earth, for her sins have reached unto heaven, and God hath remembered her iniquities."*

Where is the nation called *"Christian"* that does not permit prostitution, fornication and adultery with all their debasing, demoralizing, degenerating and corroding effects, with all their tendencies to disease and crime, to operate unchecked, and to leaven and corrode all classes of society?

Where is the *"Christian nation"* that punishes the crime of adultery and fornication with death, or other heavy penalties?

Where are the institutions which prohibit the marriage of all persons disqualified by nature, or by vicious habits and practices, to answer the ends of an institution so holy and pure?

In the holy chambers of the sanctuary in Zion, are revealed and ministered those sacred ordinances, covenants and sealings, which lay the foundation of kindred sympathies, associations, and family ties, indissoluble and eternal—ties which are stronger than death, more durable than the ramparts of their snow-clad mountains, and which will never be dissolved—

"While life, or thought, or being lasts;
Or immortality endures."

The restoration of these pure laws and practices has commenced to improve or regenerate a race. A holy and temperate life; pure morals and manners; faith, hope, charity; cheerfulness, gentleness, integrity; intellectual development, pure truth, and knowledge; and above all the operations of the divine Spirit, will produce a race more beautiful in form and

features, stronger, and more vigorous in constitution, happier in tempera-
ment and disposition, more intellectual, less vicious and better prepared
for long life and good days in their mortal sojourn.

Each succeeding generation, governed by the same principles, will
still improve, till male and female may live and multiply for a hundred
years upon the earth—

"And after death in distant spheres
The union still renew."

The eternal union of the sexes, in and after the resurrection, is mainly
for the purpose of renewing and continuing the work of procreation. In
our present or rudimental state, our offspring are in our own image, and
partake of our natures, in which are the seeds of death. In like manner,
will the offspring of immortal and celestial beings, be in the likeness and
partake of the nature of their divine parentage. Hence, such offspring will
be pure, holy, incorruptible and eternal. They will in no wise be subject
unto death, except by descending to partake of the grosser elements, in
which are the inherent properties of dissolution or death.

To descend thus and to be made subject to sorrow, pain and death, is
the only road to the resurrection, and to the higher degrees of immortality
and eternal life. It is by contrast that the intelligences appreciate and enjoy.
How shall the sweet be known without the bitter? How shall joy be appreciated without sorrow? Or, how shall life be valued, or its eternal duration
appreciated without a contact with its moral antagonist—death?

Hence, the highest degrees of eternal felicity are approached by the
straight gate, and the narrow path which leads through the dark valley of
death, a eternal mansions in the realms of endless life. This path has been
trodden by the Eternal Father, by his Son Jesus Christ, and by all the sons
and daughters of God who are exalted to a fullness of joys celestial.

As has been before remarked, the union of the sexes in the eternal
world, in the holy covenant of celestial matrimony, is peculiar to the
ordinances and ministrations of the Apostleship or Priesthood after the
order of the Son of God, or after the order of Melchizedek. The Aaronic
Priesthood, or the institutions secular to the law of Moses, seemed to have
recognized no such ordinances or eternal covenants, hence, the Jewish
ordinances of matrimony come to end by death.

Nor did the sects of the Pharisees, Sadducees, or theirs of that nation, conceive of any thing more lasting than this life, in the covenants of matrimony. Hence, the Son of God, in answer to the Sadducees, referred to the order of the angels, in the resurrection, instead of the order of the gods.

But, the Apostles, holding the keys to the eternal mysteries of God's kingdom, to seal both on earth and in heaven, understood and testified, that, "The man is not without the woman, nor the woman without the man in the Lord."

All persons who attain to the resurrection, and to salvation, without these eternal ordinances, or sealing covenants, will remain in a *single state,* in their saved condition, to all eternity, without the joys of eternal union with the other sex, and consequently without a crown, without a Kingdom, without the power to increase.